D0348928

When God Winks On Love

Also by SQuire Rushnell

*When God Winks at You: How God Speaks Directly to You
Through the Power of Coincidence*

When God Winks on XanGo: 7 Steps to be Great at Networking

*When God Winks: How the Power of Coincidence
Guides Your Life*

When God Winks On Love

Let the Power of Coincidence Lead You to Love

SQuire Rushnell

ATRIA BOOKS

New York   London   Toronto   Sydney

ATRIA BOOKS

1230 Avenue of the Americas
New York, NY 10020

ISBN-13: 978-0-7434-8892-1
ISBN-10:   0-7434-8892-X
ISBN-13: 978-0-7434-9294-2 (Pbk)
ISBN-10:   0-7434-9294-3 (Pbk)

First Atria Books trade paperback edition February 2007

10 9 8 7 6 5 4 3 2 1

ATRIA BOOKS is a trademark of Simon & Schuster, Inc.

Manufactured in the United States of America

For information about special discounts for bulk purchases,
please contact Simon & Schuster Special Sales at
1-800-456-6798 or business@simonandschuster.com.

*To my earthly guidance system—
my wonderful wife, Louise DuArt*

Acknowledgments

I am deeply grateful for the extraordinary godwink which led Marcella Clashman, a bright Waldenbooks buyer, to first mention my book to Judith Curr, the dynamic Atria Books publisher. I shall be ever thankful for Judith's quick perception, adroit leadership, and the subsequent support of her entire team. Moreover, Brenda Copeland, my sharp, charming, and enormously supportive editor at Atria Books deserves vast praise in nurturing the birth of this book.

Lastly, I acknowledge every couple whose wonderful love story is told in these pages. Their willingness to share their personal experiences will foster incalculable hope to thousands of people who deeply desire the joys of perfect love.

Dear Reader,

This book will validate your feelings that there's more to coincidence than meets the eye.

It will also foster hope for the dreams of your future by unveiling the wondrous map that has quietly guided you along the paths of your past.

God has been winking at you.

—SQuire Rushnell

P.S. Please contact me when these promises come true. Visit whengodwinks.com or write me at P.O. Box 690531, Quincy, Massachusetts 02269-9903.

P.P.S. Yes, in case you are wondering, the "Q" in my name is supposed to be capitalized.

Contents

co·in·ci·dence (ko-in'si-dens')
A sequence of events that although accidental seems to have been planned or arranged.

—American Heritage Dictionary

wink (wingk)
To give a signal or express a message.

—American Heritage Dictionary

god·wink (god'wingk')
A personal signal or message directly from a higher power, usually, but not always, in the form of a coincidence.

—the Author

Introduction

There's no coincidence to coincidence

"It's no coincidence you just opened this book. It could be a godwink."

When I first expressed that thought in the hardcover version of this book, I had no idea that it would have such a profound connection with people looking for the same answers I had once searched for, and found.

I also had no idea how many people would want to share their godwink stories with me, partly to validate their hopes that they were indeed on course to finding perfect love.

But, wait, I'm jumping ahead. I can't assume that you know what a *godwink* is.

In short: I believe that every time a coincidence happens, a prayer is answered, or something makes you shout, "Wow! What are the odds of *that* happening?" you've received a godwink. It's a signpost along your path to your destiny—a reassuring message from above, that you are never alone.

I call it a godwink because when you were a kid someone

you love—your mom, or dad, or grandma—sent you a quiet communication. A wink.

You never asked what that wink meant. You knew.

It meant: "Hey, kid, I'm thinking about you right now. Hang in there. I'm with you."

That's the same message as a godwink.

It's a simple concept, I know. And, you may be wondering *how come nobody ever put it that way before?*

Don't know. I'm just the messenger.

But I have proved to my satisfaction that this simple premise is a life-changing concept. Because once you accept the notion that you are on a sort of GPS—a Global Positioning System I like to think of as God's Positioning System—you will begin to see godwinks more and more. And the more you see them . . . the more they are there.

So, how does this apply to love?

Godwinks are like signposts on the highway. They don't tell you *where* to go . . . they are reassurances that you are following the path that *you* decided to go.

In the quest for love we always need to resist the temptation to conclude that godwinks are telling us what guy or girl is right for us. Godwinks don't *tell* us what decisions to make anymore than that wink from Grandma across the dining room table. It never directed you to "go ahead, have another piece of pie."

Instead, a godwink is a Divine arm around your shoulder at

a moment of uncertainty . . . an encourager, not a decider in the decisions you make.

And I believe that as you come into Divine alignment with the world around you, Divine things will begin happening to you.

And you *will* find perfect love!

My mission in this book is to help you to find comfort with that declaration . . . to help you really believe it. I'll do that by sharing wonderful, inspiring stories of others like you who sought perfect love and found it. And, you'll see how godwinks, as signs of encouragement, were always present. Always saying, "Hey kid . . . I'm with you."

The jigsaw puzzle of love

We all go through times when we seem to be swimming in a sea of uncertainty.

Haven't you found yourself glancing skyward, wondering, "Hey! Is anybody up there listening to me?"

Let's face it. Sometimes your life feels like a jigsaw puzzle dumped out on the dining-room table. You pick up one piece at a time and say, "I don't get it! Why doesn't this fit together?"

You ask, "What happened to that fairy tale in which I was supposed to have a starring role? Where is the love in *my life?*"

Here is what I'd like you to consider.

When you're doing a jigsaw puzzle it never enters your mind that it might not go together, does it? Of course not. You innately know that if you have the patience to keep working at it, the pieces will all go together.

For one thing, you believe in the picture on the box!

You have *faith* that, regardless of the degree of difficulty, all those little pieces are supposed to correspond perfectly. You know it's up to you to have the tenacity to keep at it. And when that puzzle is completed—and seen from above—you'll arrive at the not-too-astonishing conclusion that it was intended to fit together all along!

Now *that* is what you must believe about *your life!*

That your life is intended to fit together perfectly.

That all the right pieces are there in the pile.

That if you have faith in the outcome, the picture you've seen in your mind can be yours.

And that when your life is finally assembled, and seen from above, it *will* be perfect.

But, but, but . . . you're saying: "Am I supposed to believe that my Prince Charming or Cinderella is in that pile of pieces called "My Life"?

Yes. But it comes with this caution.

Have you ever picked up two pieces of a jigsaw puzzle that seemed like they were a perfect match? You wanted them to be a fit? So then you jammed them together to try to get them to fit? In the end, didn't you conclude, that regardless of how much you wanted them to go together, all you did by forcing them into place, was to injure each piece?

This is the primary message of this book: have patience. Have faith that the godwinks along your way will provide you with reassurances . . . serving as encouragers . . . as you put your life together.

If you're just beginning a relationship, strongly resist the temptation to jam yourself into an imperfect match. They never fit.

If you are already in an uncertain relationship, you still need patience. Dedicate enough time to be certain that you're not giving up too soon, mindful that some relationships evolve to perfection more slowly. But, in the end, remember that nowhere does it say that you were placed on this earth to be unhappy.

You have the right to God-given happiness.

1

There IS a Perfect Fit for You

Let us embark on a wonderful journey of hope.

Through breathtaking stories of romance, incredible love stories that have united or reunited people just like you, I am hopeful that you'll see your own life in a fresh new light, filled with renewed hope that your perfect love is not nearly as distant as you thought.

Through the Six Key Words to Successful Relationships that unfold in the stories of others, I believe that you will clearly see that you are on a path to finding your soul mate. Your soul mate may be already near. Perhaps you are already in a relationship that has not yet matured to soul mate status. But I am certain of this: in the grand design of your life, there is a perfect love for you.

How can I be certain?

I have spoken with hundreds of people, who, just like you, have asked "Is there someone out there for me?" People who found the answer said: "Yes."

I have also been in your shoes.

SQuire and Louise—my shoes fit you

I had never said "I Love You" without some twinge of ignorance, way down deep.

"Do I really know what love *is?*" I asked myself.

"Am I in love, infatuation, or just a desire to *be* in love?"

On those rare occasions when I entertained the *big question*—"Is this your soul mate?"—my head was mute.

Married twice, twice divorced. That was pretty much the answer.

Yes, I was indeed ignorant about love.

Attending church alone on Sunday mornings, I tried unsuccessfully to submerge my envy for a loving couple who always sat three pews ahead of me. I watched the way they would position themselves, shoulders touching, turning, smiling at each other; and the way they seemed to communicate through a secret language of eyes and body known only to themselves. Through the crowd of departing parishioners I'd watch them leaving church holding hands, providing a wonderful model for their teenaged children, not to mention the rest of us.

That couple made me realize that even though I had been

married most of my adult life, I had spent years imprisoned in loneliness. I deeply wanted what they had.

So do you.

Let me assure you: there *is* hope.

What I thought would never happen in my lifetime—that I would be the prince who someday placed the slipper on the foot of Cinderella—*did* happen! And when the perfect piece fell into place in the jigsaw puzzle of my life it arrived with a clarity comparable to every soul mate couple I have interviewed. One partner or the other almost always says, "That's the man [or the girl] I'm going to marry." They had found *the* one—and they knew immediately.

When I found myself together with Louise—thirty years after I'd serendipitously played a role in her getting into television—I knew!

Even better, so did she!

The first time I ever saw Louise DuArt, she burst onstage at Madison Square Garden with a green face and a long nose with a wart on it.

"I've since had that removed," she now says, going for the joke. What should I expect? She's a comedienne.

But back then, Louise was Witchiepoo in the Kroffts' *H. R. Puf-n-stuf* road show. She had that special stage presence that reached out and almost grabbed the audience by the lapels. She had the makings of a star!

Not long after that I was working with the Kroffts on a Saturday morning block of programs under my charge at ABC. We'd come up with the idea to create a rock group that would wrap around all of our shows. When it came to casting a comedienne, I offered, "What about the girl who played Witchiepoo?"

That was all I did. No big deal in my mind. But, from Louise's perspective, that was her first big break in TV.

Weeks later I met her for the first time, for a moment or two, at an advertiser function, and over the course of the next three decades briefly saw her at ABC affiliate events or backstage at *Good Morning America*. During each of those encounters she was married. So was I.

Several years passed.

My second marriage had broken up, and I was running a cable TV network in Washington, D.C. I had traveled to New York City to pick up my son, Grant, where he was living with his mother, to take him on a long anticipated, fun-filled weekend in Canada coinciding with a meeting I had scheduled in Toronto. But, at the last minute, the meeting was canceled. The trip had to be called off, and my son was upset.

"What do you say we stay in New York and take in a Broadway musical?" I said, trying to broker some enthusiasm.

I have learned that kids with developmental challenges, as

Grant has, seem to universally enjoy music even if they are unable to read and write.

Grant's brightness was restored when I spotted a musical in *The New York Times* called *Dreamstuff* and exclaimed that the star—Louise DuArt—was an old friend.

"Hey, maybe we can meet her backstage!"

His gloom dissipated.

After the show Grant and I met with Louise and her manager, Howie Rapp, for a cappuccino. We jibber jabbered, catching up on intervening years. When I inquired about her husband, her reply startled me.

"He left me for another woman," she said.

"Oh. I'm . . . going through a transition, myself. . . ." I stuttered, covering, as best I could, the skipping of my heart.

Perhaps my heart was just coming to realize what my mind had been denying in every previous encounter with Louise over the three previous decades. For, in retrospect, every time I'd run into her, I'd had this uplifting feeling—the kind you have just after a thunderstorm, when the air is filled with ions—soaring my spirits.

I was wondering what to make of those feelings, when a godwink became apparent. A sign of reassurance.

"What a godsend you came today," she said. "You just saw our last show. It closed."

"Really? Grant and I were supposed to be in Canada today," I quickly rejoined, "but our trip was canceled at the last minute."

We've since marveled at that godwink—the divine timing that caused our paths to intersect on that day—and how our lives continue to be monitored and mapped from above on a sort-of grand Global Positioning System that we have playfully renamed "God's Positioning System."

Later on, I found out that Louise had called her mother after our post-theater coffee, and said, "Today I met the man I'm going to marry."

A short while later, that's exactly what happened—Louise and I were married—soul mates cast in a fairy tale called "Happily Ever After."

Why did it take so long to find the perfect fit in the jigsaw puzzle of my life?

I have no idea. But Louise and I are clear about this truth we learned the hard way: that jamming together two pieces of a puzzle—no matter how much we *wanted* them to fit, in a moment of desire, or out of a false sense of obligation, never resulted in true happiness.

As Louise and I look at our lives through the long lens of time, we have to admit that God has had a lot of patience with us—*and our choices*. Perhaps it is only fair that we be expected to have patience with Him.

In the end, patience paid off.

Louise and I are perfect for each other.

And when the fit is perfect, life is perfect.

Don't expect it to be easy

We tend to forget that even in fairy tales, finding your perfect love is not easy. Cinderella had to clean a lot of chimneys and endure a lot of barbs from her stepsisters before she got to go to the ball. And even then, there was great uncertainty—she had no idea whether anyone at the ball would give her a second glance, let alone the prince. The ball was followed by the uncertainty of not really knowing if she would ever connect with the prince again. After all, he never took her phone number or email address.

Patience—that word you hated as a kid when your parents uttered it—is something we really do have to call upon.

That is particularly true if your parents are still involved in your life, trying to hurry you along toward a relationship, as occurred in the following story.

The other Hillary and Bill

Hillary Kimmelman and Bill Solomon invited Hillary and Bill Clinton to their wedding. The president and first lady couldn't make it. Not in person, anyway.

But, let's start at the beginning.

When Hillary Kimmelman broke up with her boyfriend,

her view of the future was clear: "I'm thirty-two. My life is over. I'm never going to find the perfect person."

Meanwhile, Bill Solomon had his share of dysfunctional relationships, also leaving him with a pessimistic outlook on the future.

They did not know each other.

They also did not know that forty years earlier their parents had been high school friends who had double-dated in Long Beach, Long Island. But when Hillary's father Larry, and Bill's mother Barbara, went off to college, they lost touch. Larry settled in Boston. Barbara remained on Long Island.

One day someone sent Hillary's father an article from the local Long Beach paper. It was a cooking column featuring a lady who raved about a salmon dish that she'd lovingly termed, "My son Bill's Salmon Recipe."

Larry smiled when he recognized the lady as Barbara Solomon, his high school friend. He tracked her down by phone and soon they were catching up on four decades in between. Larry and Barbara revealed that they were both still happily married, and each had grown children.

"I have a daughter who lives in New York," said Larry.

"My son Bill lives there, too," said Barbara.

"Ahhh, the son who's the salmon recipe," he laughed, recalling the newspaper article.

"Yes. He lives downtown, on Fifth Avenue."

"Really? So does Hillary."

"No kidding. What building?"

Well—believe it or not—they both lived at the same address. And while there was no way for them to know it at the time, their offspring had apartments in exactly the same location, on two different floors, seven stories apart.

Traditionally, a situation like this leaves parents with no other option: plot to get their two kids together.

"I have a Hillary and you have a Bill," observed Larry, kiddingly. "Maybe they'll marry and we can have the reception at the White House," an oblique reference to President Bill and Hillary Clinton.

They laughed.

But their children didn't.

Hillary Kimmelman accepted her mother's suggestion that she ought to meet the son of the former friend who lived in her building who had a salmon dish named after him—in the same manner as she would accept a dirty diaper.

Bill Solomon accepted his mother's notion of dating the "beautiful" daughter of an old friend of hers who lived right there in his own building, with absolute horror. Dating someone his *mother* recommended, was too awful to imagine.

Another downside immediately crossed his mind. "Having a blind date with someone from my own building meant that my apartment would no longer be a safe haven," he observed.

In response to their parents they both did exactly what you would expect.

Nothing.

Weeks later Bill was Rollerblading in nearby Union Square when he ran into a former colleague. They chatted. And then went their separate ways.

Back at his apartment building Bill encountered the former colleague again. This time she was standing in the lobby. "What are you doing here?" he asked, surprised.

"My best friend from college lives here—Hillary Kimmelman."

"What a weird coincidence. I was supposed to go on a blind date with her, but I never called her."

"Well, you should," she counseled, "She's great."

He began to wonder: should he, or shouldn't he?

Hillary's father, meanwhile, was pressing the issue. "Every time I call home, my father tortures me," she complained to a friend. "He asks, 'Has Bill-the-salmon called you yet?' "

Bill's mother was just as relentless.

Finally, Bill called Hillary and they had a surprisingly delightful conversation, discovering many mutual interests including skiing, tennis, and Rollerblading.

They made a date.

Hillary would travel seven floors down to Bill's fourth-floor apartment, then they'd go to dinner.

When the door opened, Hillary was pleasantly surprised: "He's absolutely adorable," she said to herself.

Bill was similarly stunned: "Wow, my mother was right—she really *is* beautiful."

They were both a bit nervous.

Bill handed Hillary a glass of red wine. It slipped, spilling onto the carpet. Quickly mopping it up he thought to himself, "I don't have the heart to tell her—I just had it installed today."

At a nice restaurant in the area, they placed their orders.

Hillary, struggling not to snicker, heard herself saying, "I can't believe it, he's ordering *salmon!*"

When they returned home, entering the same building, awkwardly looking at each other as one pushed the fourth floor, the other the eleventh, it seemed like a scene out of a Tom Hanks-Meg Ryan romantic comedy.

A few minutes after she got home, Hillary's phone rang. It was Bill. "I just wanted to see if you got home all right," he joked.

As Bill and Hillary began their courtship, they couldn't resist adding up the coincidences that had unfolded. In addition to their parents being childhood friends and their living in the same New York apartment building:

- They found that they had both worked for Ron Perelman companies—Hillary for Revlon, Bill for the New World TV stations;
- Both had worked in the *same office building*, 575 Fifth Avenue;

- Bill, and Hillary's father, Larry, both went to Boston University;
- At BU, Larry had a roommate who transferred to the University of Miami, where he became the roommate of *Bill's* father, Jack Solomon;
- Bill had a roommate at BU who transferred to the University of Maryland and became the roommate of a man who later was a colleague of Hillary's;
- And, if that wasn't enough, Hillary's father and Bill's father shared the *same birthday*, June 10.

As their relationship began to grow, the coincidences never escaped them.

"We kept using the words 'destiny' and 'bashert' . . . Yiddish for 'intended one,' " says Hillary.

"But today we have come to expect coincidences," finishes Bill.

For their wedding, two years after they met, Hillary and Bill decided to invite the *other* Hillary and Bill—the one's then residing in the White House. The wedding guests all loved having their pictures taken with both sets of Hillary and Bill—albeit the president and first lady were only life-size cutouts.

One additional godwink completes the circle—it connects Hillary and Bill to my wife and myself. Their story caught the attention of *New York Times* reporter Lois Smith Brady, who wrote it up for her popular "Vows" column in the Sunday paper. Coincidentally, Lois Smith Brady had also heard about my betrothal to Louise and profiled our wedding in her *Times* column.

Laughter—a step to successful relationships

Throughout this book I have asked couples for their wisdom on the most important steps to a successful relationship. One that redundantly surfaces is laughter.

Bill and Hillary found that a sense of humor was a common thread to both pull them together, and to hold them together.

Laughter, they reminded me, is also an important tool to unveil during tense moments that invariably arise in relationships: if one partner or the other can muster some humor, emotional stress is relaxed, and the potential for disagreement dissipates.

Destiny doesn't come to you—you must go for it

I believe that each of us has a destiny. It's like our DNA. It's there. We're born with it.

But I also believe that God has allowed you to have your hands on the steering wheel most of the way through life: you can go too fast, too slow, or recklessly drive off a cliff and never reach your intended destiny.

In my motivational speaking engagements I frequently hear myself repeating this premise:

"You cannot sit on your baggage, beside the road, waiting for your destiny to come to you. You must get up, get going, and leave your baggage behind. Go for what you believe to be *your* destiny, and look for all the signposts along the way—the godwinks—that are the messages of reassurance that you're on the right path."

Think about the outcome if the principals in the story that follows had not "gone for" what they believed to be their destiny.

Paula and Gary: the innkeeper's perfect pursuit

Paula was twenty-nine. She was the oldest daughter of a fine family from the tranquil suburbs of St. Louis, was schooled as a registered nurse, and subsequently met the man she would marry. In her wedding photos, she was a strikingly beautiful blond bride. Everything seemed perfect.

It was not.

The groom was a good man, but not a good husband for Paula. He was a man's man, the kind of guy who places higher priority on all-male golf outings and hanging out with the guys after work instead of nurturing his relationship with his wife.

Paula's dreams of finding Prince Charming diminished as the marriage dissolved.

She put her attention on another long-held dream—owning a gift shop—and concluded that she could combine her career ambitions with her summer vacation plans: someone referred her to a gift market wholesaler in Boston who could help her get set up in business, and she could schedule that meeting on her way home from her annual get-together with an old friend, Mary Jane, who had a home on the island of Nantucket, off the coast of Massachusetts.

Gary Conover was a dreamer, the kind who was sent home from school as a kid with a note that said he was a dreamer but made it sound like a bad word. Yet, when Gary put his mind to something, he pursued it. He finished it. And he did it right.

At the age of eleven, Gary surprised his parents when they saw what he'd done to his room: he'd redecorated and repainted it to look like a suite in an upscale inn.

He spent several post-schooling years as an insurance salesman in Philadelphia, met and married the girl of his dreams (he thought), and moved to the island of Martha's Vineyard, off the coast of Cape Cod, fifteen miles from Nantucket. He and his wife opened a small art shop in Edgartown, Massachusetts—the Vineyard's oldest, most quaint community—and began selling the works of local artists.

One of those, Ray Ellis, became one of the most prolific and famous artists in the country, further underscoring Gary's keen eye for things beautiful.

Always a visionary and a doer, Gary spotted a woefully dilapidated inn near the center of town that he envisioned could become both an inn and a more sizable art shop. He bought it, and commenced painstakingly authentic restoration to evolve a wonderfully charming old structure. It opened in 1972 as the newly renovated Charlotte Inn.

Gary and his wife had two handsome young boys. To outside observers perceiving that the Conovers were growing a model nuclear family while growing a business on Martha's Vineyard, everything was perfect.

It was not.

The marriage was never a perfect fit. They were like two pieces of that jigsaw puzzle who had jammed themselves together in a hopeful quest that, one day, they would somehow magically fit together, but never did.

The marriage dissolved.

Gary continued to work hard at running and expanding the inn. Over time, he began dating again. And to many fair ladies, he was the catch of catches: handsome, successful, and the owner of a charming inn on Martha's Vineyard, one of America's most desired destinations.

He believed in "perfect." His determination to achieve perfection in the presentation and accommodations of his inn was becoming legendary among leisure industry colleagues and the community.

But without perfect love, life was not perfect.

*   *   *

Paula traveled from St. Louis to Nantucket by plane, connecting through Boston. It was always good to see her old friend Mary Jane, who met her at the small island airport. They planned to spend three days on Nantucket, and then to do something they had talked about doing for three years running but never got around to: take a day-trip to Martha's Vineyard.

On the morning they were to leave for Martha's Vineyard, Mary Jane was called in to work at the last minute, yet insisted that Paula should go on to the Vineyard without her.

"No . . . I'll just wait till next year," said Paula.

"I insist," said Mary Jane. "I'll be good for you. And you must see Edgartown."

Mary Jane drove her to the Nantucket airport only to find that no flights were departing. The airport was fogged in. But before going back to Mary Jane's house, they decided to have breakfast at the airport coffee shop.

Gary Conover asked his son if he could borrow his car. It would be more fun, he thought, to drive his date to the Martha's Vineyard airport in a sports car. He needed to get her there for a 10 A.M. plane to Boston.

As Paula and Mary Jane finished breakfast, they received word that the fog had lifted. Paula's plane was leaving right away. Rushing to the gate, Mary Jane promised to pick Paula up when she returned to Nantucket later in the day.

"Have fun," she commanded, smiling and waving as Paula boarded the small plane.

When Paula arrived at Martha's Vineyard there were no cabs. She asked a man how to get to Edgartown.

"Well, because of the fog, cabs weren't waitin' around," drawled the man in a New England accent. Then lifting a nearby casement window, he shouted to a fellow standing beside his car outside the little terminal.

"Gary! Can you give this girl a ride to town?"

Turning back to Paula, he explained that on the island, people help each other out: "He's Gary Conover, an innkeeper in Edgartown."

Paula took one look at the handsome man dressed in khakis and a white shirt with rolled-up sleeves, standing next to a white Corvette convertible. "I could do worse," she quipped to herself.

Introductions made, Gary said he would be glad to give Paula a lift—he was just seeing a friend off on the same plane that Paula had arrived on. (It was determined sometime later, that, by coincidence, the lady friend Gary was seeing off would take the exact same seat as the one Paula sat in, to arrive.)

As Gary chatted with Paula about Edgartown and Martha's Vineyard, exuding pride for the island, he became more and more captivated by her. He enjoyed her interest in his art shop and inn, and invited her for a ride in his Boston Whaler, a classic-looking boat, over to the Chappy Beach Club on adjacent Chappaquiddick Island. After an afternoon tour of the shops and the narrow streets of Edgartown, Gary invited Paula to see the Charlotte Inn.

Paula was impressed! "I could *live* in a place like this," she said with awe.

"Why don't you stay over, we have rooms available," said Gary. "I could show you up-island tomorrow. You should see the beautiful red clay cliffs of Gay Head."

"No . . . no. I have to be back in Nantucket tonight," said Paula. "My friend is meeting me at the airport."

"You could go back tomorrow," pressed Gary.

"No . . . no . . . I couldn't."

"You know, we have fog in the evening this time of year," said Gary, "Let me check the airport."

Gary returned.

"Too bad," he said, almost smiling, "The airport is fogged in."

His heart had leaped when he'd called the airport to hear, "Sorry. All planes are grounded. A fog front has just come in."

As Paula examined the decor in her room, marveling at the detail that had gone into the selection and placement of every single item, mostly valuable antiques, she had a growing appreciation for the talents of the man into whose path she had been placed by the godwink of fog. She reflected on the day's nonstop conversation. How easy it was. How interested he was in what *she* had to say, *her* opinions. And . . . he seemed to like her sense of humor, too.

Through the years Gary Conover had developed a keen eye for the finer, beautiful things in life. He had spent years looking at paintings, at fine antiques, and other rare valuables. Long ago he had learned that when you see something of exceptional value, you must go for it. Doggedly. Don't wait. It may not be there when you come back.

Paula was neither a magnificent painting nor a priceless jewel, but she was a beautiful human being, a beautiful woman in whose company and by whose easy conversation he had been captivated for an entire day. From the moment that divinely engineered timing had placed him at the perfect place, at the perfect time, he was in love.

Paula called her friend Mary Jane on Nantucket. "We're fogged in. I have to stay the night," she said disappointedly, hoping it didn't sound transparent.

"Funny . . . it's clear as a bell here," exclaimed Mary Jane.

The next day Gary convinced Paula to remain on Martha's Vineyard for the whole day, and by midafternoon was again pressing her to stay—"just one more day."

"No . . . no . . . I *have* to go," she protested. "I don't want to, but I have to."

She explained that she had to gather her baggage in Nantucket, and then to depart for her meeting with the gift wholesaler in Boston the following morning.

Sadly, Gary drove her to the airport. Seeing Paula's plane lift into the sky gave him a deeper feeling of loss than he had ever before experienced. He stood riveted, trying to keep the small plane in focus for as long as he could, until it disappeared into the clouds.

Paula arrived at her appointment in Boston the next morning, greeting Tony the gift-market wholesaler, quickly explaining her plan to start a gift shop back in St. Louis. He offered that they could talk in the office or, seeing it was lunchtime, they could continue to talk over lunch. He suggested a restaurant, but on the way out of the building, decided to take her to a different one.

At some point during lunch, the waitress came to the table and asked if her name was Paula.

"Yes," she replied, puzzled.

"There's a phone call for you."

"Did you tell anyone where we were going for lunch?" Paula quizzically asked Tony, as she got up to go to the phone.

Tony shook his head.

"Hi, Paula, this is Gary," said the voice on the phone.

"How . . . how in the world did you track me down?" gasped Paula.

Gary explained that he had been doing some detective work all morning long, checking one wholesaler after another, until he reached the desk of one secretary who confirmed that her boss was having lunch with a pretty blond lady, and may have taken her to one of several restaurants. He kept calling until he reached the right one.

Gary then began his entreaties to Paula that instead of returning to St. Louis, she should come back to Martha's Vineyard.

"No . . . no . . . I can't," said Paula, wearing an astonished smile. "I really must go back home . . . I have dogs . . . I have commitments I need to keep. . . ."

Eventually convincing Gary that she had to stay the course, and that she really had to get back to her meeting, she returned to the table, apologetically explaining what had happened.

Paula rushed to the airport in order to catch her late-afternoon flight to St. Louis. Arriving at the gate just a few minutes before departure, she joined the line of people who were boarding. Something caught her attention. It was her name being spoken. She turned. The loudspeaker was saying her name, and telling her to pick up a courtesy phone. Fortunately, there was one right there on the wall next to where she was standing.

"Hi, Paula, it's Gary."

Breathless with surprise, and buoyant from his charm, Paula found herself repeating an all-too-familiar phrase: "No . . . no . . . I can't. I really do have to go back."

"Come back to Martha's Vineyard, just for the rest of the week," implored Gary. He explained that he had been calling the airport every ten minutes, telling them it was an emergency, and he had to reach her.

The man at the door of the plane was signaling Paula. All the other passengers had boarded the plane. "Are you coming?" he mouthed to her.

"Yes, just a minute," she mouthed back.

"You could catch another plane right back to the Vineyard," continued Gary.

"No . . . no. . . ."

"Are you coming, ma'am, or not?" the flight attendant was now insisting, having walked over to her, placing his face within inches of hers.

Paula paused. Perhaps a second. Maybe a millisecond.

"No. I am *not* coming!" she stated firmly . . . to the flight attendant.

Joy leaped within Gary's chest. "Here's what you do," he excitedly instructed. "Find your way to Butler Aviation—

those are private airplanes—a plane will be there for you in forty-five minutes."

In forty-five minutes a chartered plane rolled to the Butler hangar. Paula expected to see a pilot deplane. Instead, she felt a tingle as she saw Gary Conover climb down. He hugged Paula, and helped her climb into the plane, heading back to Martha's Vineyard.

For three days, Gary and Paula talked. They spoke, with certainty, that they were meant for each other. That powerful unseen forces were executing a design for their lives that was truly meant to be.

"How much time do you need to wrap things up in St. Louis?" asked Gary.

"Two weeks," replied Paula.

"How about one," smiled Gary.

During that one week that she was reconstructing her entire life—pulling up every thread of connection she had in St. Louis, to move to an island off the coast of Massachusetts—Gary telephoned, several times every day.

When Paula overpacked her car for the drive to Massachusetts and had no room for her dog carriers, she broke down crying.

The phone rang. It was Gary.

"I don't have any room for my little dogs," she cried, "I don't know what to do. I have to bring them with me."

"Don't worry about a thing," said Gary, calmly. "Do you have someone who can take the dogs just for tonight?"

"Yes . . . ," she said, softly holding back sniffles.

"Here's what you do. Take your dogs to your friend. Drive your car to the airport. Leave the car with valet parking. Tell them that a man named Kincade will pick it up tomorrow. Go to the ticket counter. There are prepaid tickets there for you."

Gary explained that he would send one of his workers to St. Louis the next day, have him pick up the car, pick up the dogs, and drive Paula's car back to Woods Hole, Massachusetts, and catch the car-ferry to Martha's Vineyard.

A few months later . . .

Like a romantic Cary Grant-Audrey Hepburn movie where the fog lifts, the music swells, and two soul mates embrace, Gary and Paula came together as husband and wife in a small ceremony at one of the most idyllic spots on earth: the private quarters of their very own Charlotte Inn on Martha's Vineyard. As the bride and groom looked through charming small-paned windows into a magnificent English garden, traces of mist began to emerge, a reminder that the divine maker of all things perfect is the author of perfect love. He is also the creator of perfectly timed fog—as godwinks.

*   *   *

Today, Paula looks back upon her decision with clarity: "I knew the moment I spoke those words to the flight attendant— 'No, I'm not coming'—that I was not just curtailing a trip to St. Louis. I was making a much bigger decision—the right one—for the rest of my life."

"It's amazing," says Gary, reflecting on twenty-two years of happy marriage, "In twenty-two years we've never had a single argument. We're together, running the inn, almost every moment of every day. Yet, when she goes to the grocery store, I miss her."

The difference between determination and desperation

Gary Conover was never desperate in going after what he believed to be his perfect mate. But once he saw her, and sensed that "she was the one," he *was* determined.

What can you learn from that?

When you pursue someone desperately, you give off scary signals. But when you are *determined*, you admirably demonstrate that you know what you want—and you're going for it.

It's a fine line, I know.

It goes back to caveman times; men like the pursuit, and women like to be pursued. But before embarking on pursuit, you have to ask, "Does this person want to be pursued? Are they giving me any signals?"

Paula gave Gary positive signals that she cared for him, and would like to continue the relationship, but that, unfortunately, she had other obligations.

By correctly reading the signals, Gary remained determined, never crossed the line of desperation, and demonstrated sensitivity to Paula's concerns. By taking charge and providing her with support, he became her knight in shining armor.

Fatherly advice

My adult daughters Robin and Hilary thought I was over the top when I sat them down to watch the Robert Redford film based on the best selling book *The Horse Whisperer*, the story of a man who had a remarkable ability to tame wild horses. He employed a calm, determined approach and used psychology.

"Watch what Redford does when he wants to put a saddle on that wild stallion," I noted. "As the horse rears and snorts, Redford shows continued determination. Never desperation.

"Notice his patience. Imagine if he tried to grab the horse by a leg and hold on for dear life. What would happen? The horse would be last seen crossing the horizon, right?

"Instead, when the horse bolts away, Redford places himself into a lower position, and waits for the stallion to come to *him*. That's what happens, and before long, that horse is saddled.

"No different with men," I counseled.

My daughters' eyebrows raised slightly. But I think they got the message.

Denzel and Pauletta—the match made in heaven

The first time Denzel Washington and Pauletta Pearson were in the same place at the same time was on the set of a seventies' film in New York in which they both had won parts. From a distance Pauletta curiously eyed the recent college graduate who'd been cast in the lead. Denzel was handsome and self-assured. But they had no scenes together. No conversation.

Six months passed before an opportunity arose for them to speak. By happenstance they both were invited to a party given by one of Pauletta's friends from Broadway. A conversation commenced and it was nonstop. Who knew they had so much in common?

Pauletta was charmed by Denzel's interest in what she had to say.

Denzel was taken with her engaging personality and attractiveness. "She was wearing purple with stripes," he remembers clearly.

That night a spark was ignited.

Not twenty-four hours later, an extraordinary godwink occurred.

Pauletta had friends who were appearing in a play at a

small, out-of-the-way theater in Manhattan. She decided to attend.

Quite independently, Denzel heard about the same play. He also decided to attend, slipping into his seat at the last minute after the play had already begun. But imagine the surprise on both of their faces when the lights went up at intermission and they found that—all along—they had been seated right next to each other.

What did that godwink mean in their lives?

Years later Pauletta would say, "Our whole introduction to each other felt like it was set up by the heavens."

That night, their embryonic relationship moved up a step when Pauletta invited Denzel to join her friends after the show at a cast party downtown. As they departed the theater Pauletta started for the subway. With quiet bravado, Denzel stopped her.

"Let's take a cab," he said.

"Hummm. I like his style," thought Pauletta.

But recalling his growing panic as the cab ride seemed to go on and on—well beyond his means to pay for it—Denzel now laughs at himself. "I was burning a hole in that meter with my eyes. I kept asking, 'How far did you say that party was?'"

Eventually, Denzel came clean. He admitted he didn't have enough money to cover the fare.

"I thought: 'There goes my food money for the next week,'" laughs Pauletta. "But—I still like his style."

That evening was the beginning of something big for both of them.

A few years later, they were married in Pauletta's hometown of Newton, South Carolina. Subsequently their four children have been raised in a household filled with love, where family comes first. Pauletta and Denzel have worked hard to minimize Hollywood pressures on their children—growing up in a home where their Oscar-winning father endures the travails of celebrity and tabloid distortion.

The couple credits their faith for family stability.

"Just be honest, work hard, and have faith," Denzel counsels his kids. He adds, "I used to think that what I did for a living—acting—was my life, but when we had that first child, acting became making a living, the child was life."

In large part, their values were passed on to them by their own parents.

"Paulette grew up in one of those close-knit families," says Denzel. "The kind where everybody comes to the airport to see you off. They're there on the runway with the ice cooler, the collard greens, and the chicken and potato salad. And when it's time to leave, everybody's crying, waving at the plane till they can't see it anymore. It is something to see."

A strong spiritual foundation is surely a highly significant factor in Pauletta and Denzel's matrimonial success, but they also rely on mutual respect.

What does she admire the most about her husband? Pauletta easily answers: "The way we can talk to each other about anything, his intelligence, his special qualities as a father, and the way he can take a negative and turn it into a positive."

Just as quickly Denzel can list things he loves the most about his wife: "Her strength, her friendship, and the way we laugh together."

"Denzel and I are both spiritually based," says Pauletta, always mindful that it was a powerful godwink that had once placed them side by side in a darkened theater.

Build on the rock

Building a relationship on the rock-solid foundation of mutual faith is a theme you will hear over and over in the true stories of happiness that are in this book. There is a lot to be said for a couple like Pauletta and Denzel, who can rise above the temptatio. 1s and pressures of Hollywood to have a model marriage.

Advising how to get to that place, they are unequivocal: their marriage works because it is not just between the two of them—it is a commitment of three, with God in the middle. That was reaffirmed in 1995 when Pauletta and Denzel renewed their wedding vows in a ceremony that took place in South Africa, performed by Archbishop Desmond Tutu.

Let me repeat: there IS a perfect fit for you

Take your mind back to childhood.

There you are, standing in the backyard, looking into a star-filled sky. You uttered "I wish I may, I wish I might . . ." and you *believed* that all your wishes could come true.

From that time on, every person in your life who decided they had the right to tell you what to do, said "Grow up."

Unfortunately, you listened.

You began to accept their notion of "reality"—that wishes never really come true. Wishes were for "dreamers." And "dreamers" sounded *so* negative.

But let's bring that star-filled sky back into focus.

We *do* live in a perfect universe.

Scientists say there is such perfection in the way the earth, the sun, and the stars all fit together, that if one planet had been placed in the sky just a teeny bit differently, we wouldn't be here today.

That's perfection.

Staying with the big picture, think about how almost all of life on earth is sustained by the perfect harmony of the seasons, the sun, and the cycles of life.

Now, zooming from the expanse of space, letting your

mind's eye focus in on the image of a newborn child—see those five little fingers and five tiny toes. Add five amazing senses, and you are looking at the creation of harmonious perfection.

That little person is you.

So listen to this: if perfection exists in that which is as large as the universe and as miniature as a baby's toe, why wouldn't it also be likely that God has created a perfect design for your life that includes a perfect soul mate?

In Yiddish they have a perfect word: bashert. It means "your intended one."

This is the simple truth of this book: your bashert is there, your intended one is right there in that pile of puzzle pieces called "My Life."

Have patience.

Make the right choices.

Don't jam yourself together with an imperfect match.

Postscript

A man named Paul expressed the point this way: he said, "We don't know everything, and our prophecies are not complete. But what is perfect will someday appear, and what isn't perfect will then disappear."

That was written a few thousand years ago in the Bible.

2

Godwinks Are Affirmation Signs

Imagine yourself in Chicago about to drive onto Interstate 80.

If you go west, you'll reach San Francisco.

If you take I-80 all the way east, you'll reach Boston.

It's your choice. But whichever you choose, the signs along the way will be there to guide you, affirming that you're heading in the right direction.

Signposts don't choose where you go.

You do.

But once you make your determination—the signposts are there to support your decision.

That's the role of godwinks in your life. They are signposts *affirming* that you are heading in the right direction, reassuring that you're getting closer to your goal, reminding you to stay within boundaries, and bolstering the choices *you* have made.

People frequently ask me about the choices they need to make in life. More often than not, they are questions about their love interests. When it comes to love, we all search for answers.

"Is this the right guy?"

"How can I be sure?"

"Is my relationship with this girl or guy heading in the right direction?"

"Is this 'commitment time'?"

I'm not a therapist like Dr. Phil, nor a theologian like Dr. Norman Vincent Peale. But I am an authority on godwinks. For more than a decade I have studied how these little signs of reassurance pop into people's lives, providing comforting signals that they're going the right way.

So when it comes to decisions about love, I usually bring people back to the original premise I spoke about earlier: godwinks are like the silent messages you received as a kid from Grandma across the dining-room table—quiet communications of support and reassurance—through a little wink.

That wink said: "Hey kid, I'm thinking about you right now. I love you. Hang in there."

That wink did *not* say, "Have another piece of pie." Or, "Help yourself to the mashed potatoes."

That wink was *not* a directive for you.

It was a reassuring communication of love *affirming* that

you had the support of someone who loved you, in the choices that *you* were making.

You'll see in the stories that follow, that Myra and Malcolm, and Debbie and Paul, and others, each had wonderful godwinks that *affirmed* they were on the right paths.

Myra and Malcolm—a train to bliss

"Men. They simply are not worth the effort," concluded Myra.

She'd been divorced for several years, and the decision to simply put men out of her mind and to stop the pursuit of a fairy tale love story that she was certain would never materialize was actually a big relief.

Only weeks after making that choice, Myra was on a cross-country train trip from California with her married sister, Sheila. As they sat in the lounge car, Sheila spotted a handsome man coming down the aisle. Always the matchmaker, Sheila said, "Let's invite him to join us."

"No, thank you," replied a firm-voiced Myra, rising to leave. "You invite him. I'm going to read."

An hour later Myra returned to the lounge only to find Sheila deeply in conversation with the man. Coaxed to join them, the man elegantly introduced himself to Myra simply as "Malcolm," without giving a last name.

Noting his British accent, Myra asked where in England he lived. "Maidstone," replied Malcolm.

Instantly occurring to her that her boss at the San Diego Zoological Society had just accepted a new job in England, Myra asked, "Is that near Leeds Castle?"

"Yes, it is."

"My boss just took a job there," said Myra.

"Oh my goodness," said Malcolm, suddenly looking surprised, reaching into his briefcase at his side, holding up the British newspaper he had been reading earlier.

"And this is he!"

Myra was dumbfounded. She was looking at her boss' picture on the front page of the London *Times*.

Sheila seemed to fade into the woodwork as Malcolm and Myra chatted on in spirited fashion. "How much time do you spend in America?" she asked.

"Until my wife died, we lived here," he said. "We owned a hotel in Las Vegas, in the Travelodge chain."

At that moment Myra again had a jolting revelation. Fleetingly, her mind flashed back in time to a single moment years before, when she worked for a San Diego printing company that produced business cards for hundreds of companies including the Travelodge chain. In that suspended moment, her mind focused on a frozen frame in her memory and she pictured herself looking at a particular business card, and reading the names aloud.

"Betty and Malcolm Hickman, Las Vegas . . . I wonder

what kind of people they are?" she remembered saying to herself.

Myra snapped back to the present.

"Wait," she said excitedly to Malcolm. "Your last name . . . it's Hickman. And your wife's name was Betty!"

Surprise swept across Malcolm's countenance.

"Yes!" uttered the astonished Englishman. "How could you possibly know that?"

She quickly told him about her inexplicable flashback of memory, to a single business card out of thousands and thousands her company had produced, and had no explanation as to why she would have remembered just that one.

They continued to explore other godwinks that seemed to unfold before them like extraordinary signposts.

"You must have known Scott King, the president of Travelodge," said Myra.

"Yes. Many times I attended Scott's parties aboard his yacht in San Diego Harbor—Betty and I never missed his Fourth of July party," confirmed Malcolm.

"Oh my gosh! We were at the same parties," blurted Myra, rapidly explaining that she too had attended the holiday parties during a period of time that she was dating Scott's nephew.

As the sun began to set on the cross-country train trip, Malcolm and Myra reiterated their disbelief in the godwinks that seemed to have rained down upon them in the course of this brief, initial conversation together: there was the English newspaper in Malcolm's briefcase with a front-page picture of Myra's boss; her incredible recollection of a single business card bearing Malcolm and Betty's name from the thousands and thousands of cards produced years earlier by a former employer; to the realization that they had both been in attendance at the same social events aboard a San Diego yacht.

Perhaps wondering if there were more signs to come, Myra asked, "When's your birthday?"

"January thirteenth," he answered. "When is yours?"

Upon hearing her reply, Malcolm dropped his head into his hands, hiding impending tears.

"June tenth?" he repeated, in an incredulous tone. "June tenth was the day my Bett died."

Myra and Malcolm found themselves entering center stage for an enduring love story.

"I am deeply grateful for the godwinks that brought me together with my charmingly elegant and sweet Malcolm," says Myra.

Look for the affirmations in your life

Like Myra, past hurts can sometimes cause you to close yourself off to the chance to find love in your life.

If that has happened to you, you need to let go of the past

and keep your heart and mind open to the possibilities that your perfect love will indeed turn up. Have faith that you will be given a second chance, or in my case, a third chance, to finally find your soul mate.

Of course you need to be careful not to leap too quickly into an ill-fitting relationship. So many times we think that by changing partners, we can make things better. Not so, if the partner isn't the right fit.

Before entering a serious relationship, do some serious soul-searching. Evaluate your mistakes of the past, as well as those of your past partners, and be certain that you're not repeating history. By learning from past mistakes, you will become someone's much better mate the next time.

Having said that, Myra stopped resisting her sister's urgings to meet Malcolm, and was glad that she did. Had she not stopped to talk with him, she would have missed out on years of blissful love, and the joyful companionship of a wonderful man.

She would have also missed the extraordinary godwinks that affirmed that they were on the right track.

Godwink affirmations are also very evident in the next story.

Debbie and Paul—the Beatles connection

It wasn't unusual for Paul Supnik to be in his law office on Sunday. And, after a week of travel, catching up on mail for a couple hours was a particularly good idea. At lunchtime, he stuck a packet of papers under his arm and went across the street to the Beverly Hills Gingerman restaurant where he was led to a small table near the ladies' room.

Paul was quite content with his bachelorhood, putting almost all of his time into building his career in copyright law. The time he budgeted for building relationships was hovering near zero.

Florence Lipton would have been perfectly cast as Dolly Levi, the gregarious matchmaker in *Hello Dolly*. She pardoned herself from lunch with her late-twenties' niece Debbie to go to the ladies' room. Passing Paul's table, she started a conversation, somehow assessed his marital status, and soon said, "There's someone I want you to meet."

Debbie was a reluctant participant.

She was not looking for a man.

Relocated from New York by CBS productions, she was perfectly happy with her unmarried status. But, Florence was persuasive, and within moments Debbie was seated at Paul's table—just for a moment—while Florence went to the ladies room. It was nearly an hour before Paul and Debbie noticed that Florence had never returned.

Their conversation, took them from one level to the next, as if they had known each other all along.

Paul asked where Debbie grew up. "Bergen County, New

Jersey," she replied, adding that her teenage years were consumed with an infatuation for the Beatles.

"In fact, I was the president of the Beatles Fan Club," she added, "and, got to go on the Johnny Carson show."

A moment, frozen in Paul's memory, suddenly burst open.

In a split second his mind reviewed a scene from years before: he was up late watching television—*The Tonight Show with Johnny Carson*—the camera turned to an effervescent thirteen-year-old girl identified as the Beatles Fan Club president. She said something funny—what was it?—oh yes, it made the audience laugh to hear her talk about the reaction of "young kids" to the Beatles, as if she, herself, were not also a "young kid."

Paul's mind flashed back to the present.

"I know you!" Paul jumped. "I *saw* you on Johnny Carson!" he exclaimed.

By what remarkable odds would Paul, twenty years earlier, as a West Coast teenager, recall a single moment that occurred to him while watching television?

Was this a spiritual nudge, planted deep into his memory bank, pressing him toward his eventual mate in life?

For Paul and Debbie it was a remarkable godwink of *affirmation*. It signaled that their paths were destined to merge. After only two dates—over the next two weeks—they were certain that they were soul mates.

They began planning the wedding.

Aunt Florence was at the wedding, of course. And it was there that the bride and groom learned another amusing godwink: the incorrigible matchmaker, Florence, had also introduced the aunt and uncle of one of Debbie's friends, many years earlier, in Detroit.

Godwink affirmations help with uncertainty

For Debbie and Paul there was little uncertainty. They knew they were meant for each other, and the godwinks simply underscored that. For most of us, however, we wrestle with uncertainty on matters of the heart.

If that's you, please remember that when godwinks affirm that you are on the right path, you benefit from a greater sense of certainty. And certainty alleviates uncertainty.

Now that you've seen how godwinks were affirmations for Myra and Malcolm, and Debbie and Paul, see what happens when godwinks literally emerge "by the book" in the next story.

Christopher and Marion: romance by the book

It was a nagging sense of uncertainty.

Christopher Hegarty and Marion Mike indeed had strong feelings for each other. They felt genuinely at ease in the other's company. And, yes, they believed they meant it when they said, "I love you." But the pain of their recent divorces—each occurring at almost the same time—set off caution signals that neither could ignore.

There were so many uncertainties. How they could manage living half a country apart, and how they could balance their work and family obligations, were only part of it.

Marion was a speech pathologist in Youngstown, Ohio.

Christopher was an executive trainer and speaker based in San Francisco. He lectured throughout the world on topics relating to his top-selling books, *How to Manage Your Boss*, and *7 Secrets of Leadership*.

But as their relationship deepened, Christopher and Marion's conversations drifted, tentatively, to the scary prospect of marriage.

"I think we are both pondering the same questions," remarked Christopher in one of their long distance phone calls.

"Yes. I think we are," agreed Marion.

"Maybe we'll get a sign," he joked, more serious than not.

Later that evening, Christopher remained deep in thought about the issue they had identified.

Was it love they were feeling?

When are you really sure about love?

Or marriage?

How did they know whether the emotions they had for each other were not just the feelings of relief and escape from recent pain?

Mostly, how could they overcome their fearful feelings about commitment?

For no particular reason, he stood, nearly trancelike, staring at his bookshelves. His eyes focused on a single book. He pulled it from the shelf.

"How appropriate," he thought as he read the title: *The Nature of Love.*

Randomly opening the book, Christopher began to read a section in which the author was discussing the theories of Lebanese philosopher Kahlil Gibran from his internationally renowned book *The Prophet.*

"Give your hearts, but not into each other's keeping, for only the hand of Life can contain your hearts," wrote Gibran, sending a charge of energy through Christopher. This clarified matters for him. He and Marion needed to give their hearts to each other, but jointly their commitment was to God.

He picked up the phone and called Marion.

"Marion, I just came across a book . . ." He paused, turning the book over to read the cover. ". . . *The Nature of Love.* It's about Kahlil Gibran's writings on love, God and marriage."

Christopher finished reading aloud the lines from Gibran that had resonated so clearly in his mind.

On the other end of the phone there was silence.

"Marion?"

"Yes . . . ," she replied, hesitantly. "Christopher . . . you're not going to believe this. I am, right now, holding the same book in my lap . . . *The Nature of Love* . . . and the only part of the book I have read is the part that you have just read to me!"

Chills went up each of their spines.

It was a powerful godwink.

That Christopher and Marion were reading the same book, at the same time, in search for the answer to the same question—nearly 2,000 miles apart—was an astonishing omen, to say the least. It was the affirming sign they were looking for, appearing before them like a neon billboard!

Within a couple of days their fears vanished and they decided to marry.

There was no point in waiting.

Christopher suggested a quaint church in Westminster, Pennsylvania, a small Amish town less than fifty miles from where Marion lived in Youngstown, Ohio. He immediately got on the phone to find the church and soon had the pastor's assistant on the line. The assistant got the minister to agree to perform the marriage ceremony on the day that he and Marion had settled upon: Thanksgiving Day.

Less than three weeks later, the small entourage from Youngstown descended upon the Westminster church, arriving twenty minutes late due to unexpected delays.

"Do you want to rehearse?" the pastor privately asked Christopher.

"No, No . . . ," replied Christopher, somewhat embarrassed that their tardiness was keeping the pastor from his own holiday celebrations of the day.

The ceremony commenced.

Glancing at Marion, Christopher winked when he heard the words the pastor had selected.

Give your hearts, but not into each other's keeping.
For only the hand of Life can contain your hearts.
And stand together, yet not too near together:
For the pillars of the temple stand apart,
And the oak tree and the cypress grow not in each other's
shadow.

Marion smiled back at Christopher.

"I now pronounce you man and wife," concluded the pastor.

To the congratulations of family and friends, Christopher and Marion left the little church.

"That was very nice of you," said Christopher, knowingly looking at Marion.

A quizzical look was her response.

"Calling the pastor," he prompted, "having him read that Kahlil Gibran passage as part of the vows."

"I never spoke to the minister," said a surprised Marion. "I thought *you* did that!"

The couple stopped.

They looked blankly at each other.

Slowly shaking their heads, each was simultaneously absorbing the enormity of the godwink—the affirming power of the godwink that reassured them that they were on the right path.

What are the mathematical odds that the very passage they had both been reading in a book, at the same time—Marion in Ohio and Christopher in California—was the same passage that the pastor of a small Pennsylvania church would select as part of their wedding ceremony?

Are you getting my point? Godwinks are affirmations in your life.

Here's a story with a smaller signpost, but carrying the same big message.

Charlie's calendar girl Molly

Charlie Lyon was twenty-three. It was time to take charge of his life.

New Year's Day was the perfect time for a responsible young man, in his final year of college, to begin planning—to set some goals.

Something he'd heard rang in his mind: "If you fail to plan, plan to fail."

Finding the right girl, getting married, and settling down, should be right there at the top, he ventured.

Another quote ran through his mind: "A goal not written is only a wish."

So, Charlie Lyon reached for his brand new calendar for the year. He paged through to August. That would be the end of the summer term and at the completion of his studies for a master's degree.

"Humm . . . that's about eight months," he calculated. "That'll be my goal . . . not to be married . . . just to know that I am adequately prepared to assume those responsibilities."

In pencil, he circled the third Saturday of the month of August, the 18th.

He closed the calendar with a sense of satisfaction: New Year's resolutions done and put away.

Charlie had not been dating anyone steadily. He had one date with a new girl, Molly, but his primary focus of late was to complete his studies.

But over the next few months, Charlie and Molly began dating more and more. He liked her. Really liked her. But by the end of June, Molly was beginning to worry that maybe they were getting too serious, too soon.

"I think we should test our feelings for each other," she suggested. "Let's only see each other every two weeks."

Charlie reluctantly went along.

During the second week of August, Charlie met Molly for their "two-week" date. Upon returning her home, they chatted for a few minutes. Simultaneously, in Charlie's mind, an incessant conversation was taking place.

"Ask her to marry you," said one side of his mind.

"No. It's too soon," said the other.

"Ask her."

"Oh . . . okay."

Standing in the living room, Charlie just "popped the question." He asked her to marry him.

Slightly stunned by his unexpected proposal, Molly looked at Charlie.

"I need to think about it," she finally replied.

"Okay."

She continued to look at him for a long moment, then said, "I'll be right back."

Molly left the room.

Charlie wondered *how much* time she needed to think about it.

"Would a week be enough time?" he asked Molly when she returned.

"Yes," she smiled. "I'll let you know, a week from Saturday."

Charlie pulled his day planner from his pocket and located one week from Saturday. As he wrote "date with Molly" in the calendar, Charlie noticed something that made him jump inside—something he'd forgotten all about. The date, August 18, was faintly circled in pencil.

On the appointed day, Charlie and Molly met for their "date." Molly greeted him with the only word he wanted to hear: "Yes."

He couldn't wait to tell her what a godwink her response had been—that the very date that he had randomly chosen eight months earlier as his goal to be prepared to accept the responsibilities of marriage, was the day that Charlie and Molly became engaged to be married.

Only two months later, they held hands across the altar and exchanged vows.

"If there truly is such a thing as a 'soul mate,' she was, and is, mine . . . even to this day," says Charlie, more than twenty-four years and seven children later.

I love these stories, don't you! They provide us with such a clear perspective about matters of love.

Some are serious. Others are downright humorous. Such as the next one . . .

Alice and Nelson's sign of reassurance

Like so many other young brides, Alice Archer was naturally nervous about her impending wedding, just two weeks away. So many questions raced through her mind.

With an unusually high rainfall that spring, would torrents of rain pour down and spoil everything?

Would her mother behave herself and not interfere—both in the wedding plans and in her new marriage?

Was she making the right choice in marrying Nelson Cogsworth, anyway?

His family, owners of a small butcher shop in Wigan, just outside London, seemed nice enough, and he seemed to enjoy his father's business. But would the betrothal of the daughter of the former mayor of Wigan to the son of the butcher foster a storybook marriage?

Just as Alice was feeling the most uncertain, a wonderful godwink took place. A simple thing, actually, but a coincidence so extraordinary that its message of reassurance could only have been heaven-sent.

A sign, encased in a picture frame, had hung in the front window of Nelson's father's small shop for twenty years stating that the shop was closed on Sundays. Two weeks before the wedding Nelson's father took it down for some repair. Disassembling the frame he found an old photograph buried underneath, in the backing. It was a picture of a man holding a small child.

When Nelson showed the photo to Alice, her heart leapt.

Written on the back were the names of the two people: they were Alice's *own* father, mayor of Wigan, holding *her* at age two.

This was literally the sign—the godwink—that Alice had hoped for. A signal from above that everything was going to be just fine.

And it was. The wedding—and the marriage—went off without a hitch.

Common denominators

Here's what you have in common with Alice and Nelson. . . .

Myra and Malcolm . . .

Debbie and Paul . . .

Christopher and Marion . . .

and Charlie and Molly.

Just as they did, you have godwinks occurring in your life—signposts of affirmation that you're on the right path.

And in the same way that their godwinks made no decisions for them, but instead reaffirmed the choices *they* had made, you have to make your own decisions in life. Just as the wink you received from Grandma was not a directive, but a sign of support—"Hey kid, I'm thinking about you, right now"—the godwinks you receive are also indicators of affirmation and support for the choices you make with your own free will.

The need for certainty

Most of the principals in these stories also desired something you want: certainty. A primary human need is certainty.

We need to feel certain that we are safe. It's when we're uncertain about our safety that we worry.

We need to feel certain that we will not lose our source of income. If we're uncertain, we worry.

And, we all desire the certainty and security of someone to love . . . someone who equally loves us. When our perfect match has not yet materialized, we are uncertain, and it's worrisome.

But the signs of affirmation that come with godwinks will help you eradicate uncertainty and worry. Often the signs are right there in front of you and you fail to see them. In your daily life, your mind can become so clouded with anxiety that you totally miss seeing the reaffirming signs of encouragement.

Try to consciously take a daily moment from your fast-track life to reassess the godwinks that may have been there, that you didn't notice. Or worse, that you noticed, but shrugged off. Ask yourself:

- Was there someone you met today, this week, or this month you wouldn't have met if you hadn't experienced a godwink?
- Did you have a coincidence or answered prayer that you may have overlooked, that now, by hindsight, might alleviate some of your worry?
- Conversely, is there a particularly nettlesome uncertainty in your life that a godwink could convert to a state of greater certainty? Be on the lookout for it.

As you begin to take better note of godwinks in your life, you will begin to see that uncertainty can be replaced by an increased sense of certainty. For godwinks are signs of affirmation: "Hey kid, you're going to be okay. You're on the right track."

3

When Godwinks Are Prayers Answered

As far as I have been able to determine—searching dictionaries, books, and asking experts—there is no word in the English language for "answered prayer."

"Prayer" is an outgoing request.

But what do you call the incoming response . . . the *answer* to your prayer?

Thank goodness . . . we now have a word: godwink.

I have contended all along that a godwink is answered prayer, another name for coincidence, or one of those things that makes you say, "Wow, what are the odds of that happening?"

What is prayer, other than communication—verbally or silently uttered to God—either consciously or unconsciously?

I know. There have been plenty of times when you have

looked skyward and said, "Hellloooo. Is this microphone on? Is anybody listening up there?"

Then it crosses your mind: "How can my request ever get through? There are six billion people on this planet jamming up the lines to heaven! How can God possibly hear everybody's request at the same time, let alone act on them?"

Well . . . because . . . He's God! That's why.

And don't ask me *how* He does it. All I know is that there are thousands and thousands of stories, all through time, that prove that prayers *are* answered. It's that simple.

But sometimes we feel as though we have to ask "*How* could He possibly do it?"

Frankly, there are many things in life we can apply that question to. I have been in the television and radio business for four decades, but I don't know *how* those pictures and voices can travel invisibly through the air, thousands of miles, and get picked up on a little box in your living room!

I have no idea *how* my microwave works. *How* my car runs. Or even *how* the toilet flushes. But when we have *proof* that they *do* work, we accept those mysteries, and get on with life.

There has been extensive research, reported in distinguished medical journals, that the people who pray about a medical crisis have a significantly higher recovery rate than those who don't.

Some studies investigating the power of prayer indicate

greater recovery rates for AIDS and cancer patients who didn't even know they were being prayed for.

If I am therefore going under the doctor's scalpel, you can bet I'll give prayer all that I have.

Most biblical experts will agree that when you pray you need to *believe* that prayers will be answered; you need to hold an *expectation* that your prayers will come true. But sometimes prayers are answered—particularly in matters of love—whether you consciously or unconsciously articulate them.

See what I mean in the four stories that follow.

Ray and Melanie: no wall stops prayerful thought

Stupid was not the word for it. It wasn't big enough.

Every time Ray Materson played those days over in his mind, starting with the day he and his one-time partner, strung out on drugs, stole a toy gun and decided to rob a bunch of people in grocery store parking lots for a measly 300 bucks—that was *more* than stupid.

That was stupid, maybe times a hundred.

What did it get him?

Prison.

He hated it. The idea that he would spend every day of the next fifteen years in a cinder-block room, not much bigger than a walk-in closet, hearing nothing but steel doors banging, inmates hollering, and a drone of heavy metal and salsa music on radios, was nauseating.

Every day ticked by under a dark cloud of fear. Inmate chatter was always about violence, hatred, and perversity. He felt a constant uncertainty that another convict—angry, fed-up, or bored—would suddenly inflict pain on him.

During the first twelve months or so, Ray tried to emulate the attitude of those around him. A chip on his shoulder. To fit in, he tried acting like a rebel outlaw, talking about gangsters, and bragging about what a tough guy he was.

Then he came to that day, alone in his cell, reading the little Bible somebody gave him, that he quietly wept.

The verse that got him was this: "The thief shall steal no more, but shall do something useful with his hands."

He realized that he needed to come to terms with himself. He had to look himself in the eye and be truthful. Admit that he had done something very, very wrong, and deserved his punishment.

He squeezed his hands into a tight clasp, and began to confess and pray.

"Lord, I have been so wrong. I have wronged other people. I don't know how You can do this, Lord, but please help me get out."

A notion came into his mind to take a new tack. He lay back on his bunk and began to re-create what it was like to be free. He thought about his mom. He remembered how hard she worked to make their home clean and attractive. He thought about visits from his grandmother. He tried to see himself as a kid walking into the room where Grandma Hattie was sitting, watching how she threaded an embroidery needle and made wonderful little flowers on doilies.

He started thinking about his favorite fall pastime, going to the University of Michigan games in Ann Arbor. He chortled at the thought that the football stadium was called "The Big House." He imagined his team taking the field, dressed in jerseys of yellow/maize and navy blue.

He thought about the upcoming Rose Bowl game—his University of Michigan Wolverines were taking on USC. He imagined himself watching the game in his cell, on a small black-and-white set from the TV loaner program. Maybe he could buy some popcorn and Kool Aid from the prison store. He wished he had a U of M hat to wear—with the school colors, yellow/maize and navy blue.

At that second Ray glanced up to see an inmate, two cells away, hanging his undergarments out to dry. Hanging on the bars were a pair of socks with stripes—coincidentally, the same colors as his home team's: yellow and blue.

A thought entered his mind. ". . . the thief . . . steal no more . . . something useful with his hands . . ."

He arranged a negotiation with the other prisoner—a pack of cigarettes in trade for the socks. He disassembled them, thread by thread. With Grandma Hattie in mind he asked the guard if he could borrow the cell-block sewing box and duplicated his grandmother's technique of threading a needle. He started to embroider a block letter—M. It was blue, outlined in yellow. Later, he took elastic from the waistband of his boxer shorts, sewed it to cloth wrapped around a piece of cardboard—creating a visor—onto which he sewed the letter M.

Now he was ready. He could watch the Rose Bowl game in style.

He wore his U of M visor cap daily. Other prisoners admired it. They asked if he could make them an emblem for their favorite team, giving him socks and other items with different colored threads. Then, every day, for months, Ray would work from first lights on, till lights out, fulfilling orders—other team logos, Harley emblems, Puerto Rican flags. Soon he had true wealth in prison currency. He had stacks of cigarette packages in his cell.

He noticed he was also getting something else from fellow inmates: *respect*. They had begun to see him as someone a little more special—with a unique talent. Moreover, he felt a sense of purpose. A new inner pride, that he was doing something worthwhile.

When an older prisoner gave him a book about Impressionist paintings, Ray began to think that maybe he could do more than just block letters and emblems. Perhaps he could create pictures with embroidery. First he did scenes from Shakespeare. Then, Bible scenes. Then images inspired by songs, and his own life.

His sister, who lived two hours away in Albany, New York, volunteered to see if she could take some of Ray's art work and get it displayed somewhere, in art shows or art shops. When she sold three pieces for about $200 each, twenty times the prison value, he was thrilled.

All during this period, Ray was growing spiritually. It never escaped him that within moments of his pleadings to God to forgive him for past behavior, and his prayer for a way out of prison, that his life in prison began to get better. That seconds after he had imagined his grandmother's embroidery, his thoughts were turned to his favorite team's school colors, then, nearly simultaneously, he saw the same colors hanging on nearby cell bars. And that an extraordinary godwink had opened his mind to the idea of combining the embroidery and colors in a productive way.

"As I worked on my embroidery, twelve hours a day, I found myself 'talking' to God," says Ray, "I expressed gratitude and asked for continued guidance."

With a tone of disbelief, he said, "I know this was absurd . . . but I asked the Almighty for something else: to please bring me someone special—a woman into my life."

Melanie Hohman was beginning to pull herself out of the pits of stress and depression that had led her into the dark depths of alcohol addiction. She began attending Alcoholic Anonymous meetings in Albany, New York. But that was problematic, too; she hated that they expected her to stand up and talk about herself and her personal issues, to everyone in the group. She was very uncomfortable in expressing herself in that manner. She was too ashamed.

Fortunately, before giving up, Melanie met a nice lady who befriended her. She invited Melanie to come to her house. There, they could talk things through, more privately.

As Melanie entered the lady's home, something extraordinarily odd happened.

"My eyes were drawn across the room to a small frame of art. It was so strange. Everything else seemed to melt away— the only thing I could see was that piece of art. I actually became physically dizzy, as a result," described Melanie.

The woman told Melanie that she was looking at her brother's artwork, an embroidery of Don Quixote, lance drawn, astride his horse. She explained how he had developed his talent in prison using the thread of socks for artistic embroidery.

Long after she returned home. Melanie remained preoccupied with the experience. What circumstances would bring a man to create such beautiful images from scraps of cloth and threads of socks? The art reflecting the artist's personal life expressed an emotional state with which she could relate. She emphathized with how lonely it must have been for him.

Melanie sat down and wrote a letter to Ray Materson, in

care of Connecticut Correctional Institution, Somers, Connecticut. Somehow, in that letter, and in subsequent letters, Melanie was able to convey what was on her mind—something she could not do in front of a group of people at AA.

September 10.

That was the day the guard passed Ray Materson a letter in a lavender envelope.

"Letter from your girlfriend, Matty?"

"I couldn't imagine who would have sent me that letter," said Ray. "I read it over and over and over again."

It was from a lady who said she had met his sister.

"It was written like she was having a conversation with me," Ray continued. "She said she was a performance artist and musician who enjoyed writing and creating—all the things that were special to me, too."

Ray didn't dare, at that moment, to think that his prayer, so recently articulated—"please bring someone special, a woman into my life"—had been answered. But he became increasingly secure with that notion as he and Melanie exchanged dozens of letters over the next few months. Each one, a conversation.

"As Christmas approached, I was feeling bad that Ray had to spend it in prison," says Melanie. "That's when I decided to visit him for the first time."

The bus ride to the prison in Somers made her feel like she was in an old movie.

"I'd never visited a prison before," she said. "When I arrived, I had to go in to maximum security; through three checkpoints, and seven steel doors. I was a wreck before I got to the place where I would meet Ray—a sterile room with long tables—inmates on one side, visitors on the other."

"I put on my best prison uniform," says Ray, "And then I saw Mel. Gorgeous. Chestnut-brown hair. She had a radiant look!"

As he approached her, it finally sunk in: "I had no idea what a big answer I was getting to my prayer. At that moment I *really* knew. I looked up and said, 'Thank you, Lord.' "

"Was I in love?" repeats Melanie. "Let's say there was a twinkle at that first meeting. A spark. I'm pretty suspicious . . . I like to walk around something before I decide how I feel. But . . . there was chemistry."

"I was in love," says Ray. "No question about it."

Over the course of the next three years, Ray and Melanie corresponded with great regularity. The letters helped Ray to break the loneliness of prison. And written communication—

the ease of saying things on paper, rather than speaking—was helping Melanie to heal as well. She had beaten her addiction to alcohol.

Once, while talking about Ray's art, she said, "You ought to be represented. You should have art shows."

"Why don't *you* represent me?" he replied.

"You gotta be kidding!"

He wasn't.

She went to the library, checked out several books on the matter, and began representing Ray's artwork. She developed a theme that worked very effectively: "Art can heal. Through the creative process a person can repair years of damage."

They maintained their personal, and now business relationship, through a constant flow of letters. Occasionally Melanie would make the trip to Somers prison. On almost their third anniversary of having met, Ray greeted her with a surprise.

Ray had improved his status in many ways. Due to good behavior he was moved from maximum security to minimum. He had painted a mural for the warden, which didn't hurt his standing as a prisoner. And, he had been enthusiastically supported by a local pastor, Doug VanderWall, of the Avery Street Christian Reformed Church.

In a secret pact with Doug, Ray had arranged for a check

he was due from a particular art dealer to be sent, not to Melanie, but directly to Doug. With that money, he would buy a diamond ring.

On the December day Melanie was to arrive at the prison, Ray had arranged a special dispensation from the warden to have two visitors simultaneously: Melanie and Doug. Melanie was let in first. Then Doug, who slipped a small, preapproved box to Ray.

Right there in the visitors' room, Ray knelt down on one knee, opened the box, and said: "I love you Melanie. Will you marry me?"

Melanie was surprised. She thought it unusual that rules had been broken—that Pastor Doug was there at the same time. But, there was no hesitancy. She said, "Yes."

"Forget about privacy. It was like proposing in a bus station," snapped Ray, wittily.

A prison wedding was arranged for four months later. With Pastor Doug VanderWall presiding, Ray and Melanie Materson took their vows in a prison conference room, and were permitted twenty-four hours in a honeymoon trailer.

It was two more years before Ray was granted his freedom. He had served half of his fifteen-year sentence.

Today Ray and Melanie share their lives with three children—two of their own, and Melanie's from a previous marriage—and Ray supplements his art career by serving as a counselor at a residential youth facility. His counsel for kids to follow the straight and narrow path through life resonates more powerfully to young people because of his own past experiences.

Melanie, who works part-time at their church, received a scholarship to complete a bachelor's degree in Fine Art. In addition to continuing to represent her husband's art, she plans to teach art at the college level.

Rarely does a day go by that Ray does not look heavenward and express his thanks for the extraordinary godwinks he experienced. When he uttered the prayer, "I don't know how you can do this, Lord, but please help me get out," he could never have imagined that thoughts about his favorite team's school colors would parallel another man hanging yellow and blue socks on a railing. When he uttered another prayer: ". . . please bring me someone special—a woman into my life," he could never have imagined how he would meet his soul mate behind the prison walls.

Melanie too, expresses her gratitude to the powerful forces that directed her path—from alcohol dependency, to the man, locked behind concrete blocks, that she fell in love with and married.

"Providence brought us together," she muses.

If Ray's prayers were heard, from a place where he felt total helplessness and isolation, why can't yours be heard, too?

They can.

Although you often will receive something other than what you prayed for, I have never known it to be worse—it has always been better than expected.

Ray's prayer was *consciously* articulated.

In the next story, the prayer was stated unconsciously.

Middy's love of nature

Middy had a ritual about the *Houston Post:* every Saturday morning she'd get the paper, grab a cup of coffee, climb back into bed, and read it cover to cover—always saving her favorite column for last: "The Texas Naturalist."

"It was written by a veterinarian, Dr. B. C. Robison," said Middy. "He wrote beautifully about bugs and bunnies. And once in a while, he'd mention 'the wife.'" Reflectively, she added, "I once had a thought: 'That woman is so lucky. Wouldn't it be wonderful to be married to a guy like that— who loves animals and nature.'"

Middy Randerson was going through one of the valleys of life. At thirty-two her mismatched marriage was off the track and long devoid of romance.

She mustered the courage to end her marriage only to find herself encountering the uncertainties of unemployment. She was suddenly laid off from her public relations job.

Middy concluded that she was still stuck in a valley of misfortune when an interim job at a Christian bookstore fizzled. The store went out of business.

Yet, only by hindsight can she now see that the closing of the bookstore was really an unexpected blessing. It was a godwink causing her to open another door, to knock just one more time on a door that had failed to open on five previous attempts: her application as a reporter for the *Houston Post*. Every time she applied, there were no openings. But on the sixth time the door of opportunity opened. She got a job.

Things were looking up. Particularly so when she glanced up from her desk during her first week at the paper to see a man greeted by others with familiar joviality. Middy recognized the man from his picture in the paper. He was the freelance writer of her favorite column—"The Texas Naturalist"— Dr. B. C. Robison, routinely dropping off his column for the Saturday paper.

Without hesitation, Middy walked up to Dr. Robison and introduced herself as a longtime fan.

Over the next few months, breezy chats between Middy and B.C. led her to understand that B.C. was no longer married. And, one day, in a spur-of-the-moment-sounding invitation, B.C. said, "Let's go to lunch Sunday."

On that memorable day—September 16—Middy and B.C. headed for lunch after attending a church service. Crossing the street, B.C. spotted a dog that appeared lost.

"That's somebody's pet," said B.C., noting an identifying collar. "We can drop him off with a vet I know. They can get him home."

"You just have to fall in love with a man who prays with you and then picks up a stray dog on your first date," says Middy with a smile.

Middy and B.C. were engaged within two weeks. Except for the six-month waiting period required by the Episcopal Church, they would have been married in another two weeks.

For Middy Randerson, it is still a fairy tale come true. And, from her memory, she can summon with absolute clarity that single moment years before—while reading her Saturday morning paper—that she said: "Wouldn't it be wonderful to be married to a guy who loves animals and nature."

One wonders: was Middy unconsciously uttering a prayer?

This we *do* know: it was answered.

Nichole and Jess—the love of my life (literally)

Nicole had never been to a NASCAR race. But when she was invited by a friend from work she thought it might do her some good; perhaps she could drown her worries in the cacophony of forty-three souped-up cars roaring past a cheering crowd of 125,000 people.

Her health had been getting worse and worse.

Several years before, she'd been diagnosed with a rare liver ailment. As it progressed, the doctors said she would need a transplant in order to survive. The new liver would need to come from a live donor who was both willing and able to donate 60 percent of their own liver. Unlike brain-dead donors, the live donor had to be someone with whom she was "emotionally connected"—a family member, for instance. They had to have the same blood type, the same size liver, and their medical history had to be devoid of surgery. In short—they had to be in perfect health.

Weighing on Nicole's mind was that each member of her family had volunteered to be a donor, but failed to meet the test criteria. The clock was ticking. Physically, she was feeling weaker and weaker. Fatigue was increasing and jaundice—a yellowing of the skin—was becoming more apparent.

The noise and excitement of prerace activity at the Phoenix International Raceway was a good distraction. The friend who had invited her was affable and started an easy conversation with the fellow in the next seat.

Nicole glanced at the man. There was something familiar about him. Her friend asked the man where he was from.

"About nine hundred miles from here—Carlin, Nevada," he replied.

"That's where she's from," said Nicole's companion, nodding in her direction.

They introduced themselves. He was Jess Coleman. She, Nicole Munda.

"I know you!" exclaimed Jess. "I ride in a carpool with your mom every day to the gold mine."

She faintly recognized him as someone from their mutual hometown in northern Nevada. As they began to talk, they seemed to have quite a bit in common. From Jess's daily chats with Nicole's mother on their way to work, he knew all about Nicole's health crisis.

"How are you feeling?" he asked with an earnest sincerity. "Have you gotten any closer to finding a donor?"

She shook her head, surprised that he would know so much about her medical condition.

As their conversation continued, they learned more things they had in common: they both had backgrounds in criminal justice. She worked in the coroner's office and he had once been a police officer.

A thought of something else they had in common suddenly came to Jess: "Hey, I've got your picture on my wall," he exclaimed. He was remembering the time that Nicole and he had been in a group of people who had gone white-water rafting. A picture of that event was proudly framed and hung on his wall.

As Jess spoke, seeing him at the rafting outing began to faintly rise in her memory, but she could recall no conversation.

She and Jess lightly observed that it was interesting that they would have both been on a rafting trip in Carlin, and then turn up nearly one thousand miles away, in Phoenix, seated next to each other in a stadium of 125 thousand people.

Nearly forgetting about the companions they were with,

the two had plenty to talk about. Somewhere in their conversation they exchanged telephone numbers.

Three weeks later Nicole and Jess had their first phone conversation. "Then, we just never stopped talking," said Jess. "We talked every day after that. We love talking."

Jess had been married once before and swore he'd never do it again. But, here he was, comfortably finding himself talking with Nicole about *marriage*.

The point they actually *decided* to get married, said Nicole, "was when we realized we were finishing each other's sentences."

Seven months after their serendipitous racetrack meeting, Nicole and Jess were married in a small, family-and-close-friends-only ceremony.

The first order of business for the newlyweds: an assessment of Nicole's health. That required forgoing a honeymoon and traveling, instead, back to Phoenix to see a battery of doctors.

The news couldn't have been worse.

Doctors told Nicole that tests indicated that she might have cancer of the liver. She probably had six months to live.

Oh, no!

In the infancy of their marriage, it is hard to imagine what raced through Nicole and Jess's minds! Was there any way to repair the dreams that had suddenly been shattered? Did they have the deep levels of faith that seemed necessary at that moment?

"My primary job was to make her well," said Jess in a voice that was determined. "I told Nicole, 'We just aren't going to lose you.' "

The doctors explained the only way they could be certain whether cancer had invaded the liver was by removing and testing it. But to do that, they would need an appropriate donor for a *new* liver. And up until then, none could be found.

"How about testing me," said Jess, quickly realizing that as her new husband he certainly met the "emotionally connected" criterion.

The doctors agreed to try.

They tested his blood type. Perfect. It was the same as Nicole's.

They ascertained the size of his liver. Perfect. Same as Nicole's.

Weight and physical condition? Perfect.

Recent surgeries? Perfect. There were none.

Having passed the top-line questioning, Jess was ready to be hospitalized for one entire week of additional strenuous testing.

At week's end, the doctors' report came back. Jess *could* be Nicole's donor.

In less than six weeks after Jess and Nicole were married, the couple entered Mayo Hospital in Scottsdale, Arizona, for transplant surgery. The doctors' first task: remove Nicole's liver for cancer testing. The test came back, as an answer to prayer—a marvelous godwink—Nicole did *not* have cancer!

The second task: Jess entered surgery. Doctors removed 60 percent of his liver and transplanted it to Nicole.

Within eight hours doctors reported just what the newlyweds wanted to hear: "Both patients are just fine."

Nicole and Jess Coleman chuckle when they continue to finish each other's sentences. And they look forward to the next positive news from doctors: that Nicole's health is sufficiently repaired for her to attempt pregnancy. They have already experienced enough godwinks to last a lifetime; yet, fortunately, their path to a long, happy future has only just begun.

I asked Nicole what she believed were the three most important factors to having, and holding, perfect love:

1. "Trust."
2. "Humor."
3. "Understanding each other."

Asked separately, Jess answered:

1. "Honesty with each other."
2. "Having things in common."
3. "Faith. I never believed in faith. Then it was demonstrated to me in such a powerful way."

Arvella and Robert Schuller: in love and work

"When you get ready to be serious about a girl, start with your head, and your heart will follow, Bob."

These unsolicited words of advice from Robert Schuller's psychology professor, two weeks before the end of the school year, left the young seminary student somewhat puzzled as he watched his instructor disappear down the hall.

"What brought that on?" he wondered.

But it was good advice, nonetheless. He thought about it again and again in the days that followed, because finding his perfect mate in life was now something that seemed to dominate Robert's thinking. He decided to pray about it.

"Tell me the kind of woman I should marry, Lord, who can help me become a good preacher."

It came into his heart that he could measure his feelings about a girl by asking two questions: "Do I respect her? And, do I trust her?"

That summer Robert Schuller had landed an intern opportunity at a fledging church in Preston, Minnesota. He had one week off before taking the job, so, on the way, he decided to stop home to visit his family in Newkirk, Iowa.

Shortly after enthusiastically telling his mom and dad that he'd be leaving soon for his summer job, the phone rang. It was an elder from the church in Minnesota.

"Mr. Schuller, could we ask you to delay your arrival for one week, please? We're not quite ready for you," said the man.

"No problem," said Robert, hiding a slight disappointment.

A moment later the phone rang again. This time it was an elder from the church he'd attended as a child, right there in Newkirk.

"We hear you're in town, Bob. Could you preach for us this Sunday?"

"Well, I'd love to," said Robert, brightly. His disappointment from the earlier phone call vanished. The chance to preach his very first public, formal sermon at his own church, in his own hometown, would be an extraordinary honor. Not to mention the pride he knew this would give his mom and dad. In fact, when Robert told them the news, he noticed his dad had the glint of a tear in his eye.

On Sunday morning Robert couldn't risk being a moment late for his big debut. He arrived at the little church before any other cars were parked there. He decided to take a few minutes to meditate and look over his notes.

Fond childhood memories danced through his mind as he looked up at the bell tower of the stout, white church. Across the road he could see himself coming down the steps of his high school, remembering his perspective of looking across at the country church. Perhaps, somehow, as a student there, he was foreseeing this day—his very first day as a preacher.

A car door slammed.

A car had pulled into the church parking lot, and a slender young woman with long auburn hair was briskly walking to the back door of the church.

Robert went inside, quivering slightly.

There she was. Alone. Striking. Confident. Radiating an aura of intelligence and friendliness.

"Hi. I'm Arvella DeHann. I'm your organist today," she stated commandingly. "What hymns have you chosen?"

He stood, almost dumbstruck, looking into her smiling green eyes. Then, after an oddly long pause, he told her what he'd planned.

"Time for the prelude." She smiled again, turning quickly, "See you later."

As Robert Schuller delivered his threshold sermon as a new preacher, he couldn't help but focus on the beautiful, auburn-haired, green-eyed organist. Looking at her seemed to bolster his vigor.

At the end of the service, he was swarmed by many old friends and new ones, each offering their congratulations. He was particularly pleased that his mom and dad were also receiving congratulations. It thrilled him that he could make them so proud of their son.

Meanwhile, Robert was surreptitiously looking around,

trying to see if Arvella was still there. But when he finished shaking hands, she was gone.

"Who *was* she?" he wondered. "How come I never knew her before? How could I meet her again?"

That afternoon he called an old schoolmate, who told him that Arvella was the younger sister of another of their classmates, John DeHann.

The next day, Robert drove four miles out to Arvella's farm, under the pretense that he would say "hello" to her brother John. Mrs. DeHann invited him in, and explained that John was off to college in Des Moines. Just then, Arvella bounced downstairs, and headed for the front door.

"Hi. Good sermon yesterday. Sorry, but I've got to get to town."

She was gone again.

"I've got to go, too, Mrs. DeHann," said Robert quickly. "Tell John I said hello."

The dust from Arvella's car was rising from the long dirt driveway.

Sprinting to his car, Robert followed. She was briskly heading into Newkirk. Then, pulling in front of a store, both threw their car doors open simultaneously.

They laughed. She was on to him.

"I'm preaching again on Sunday—in Sheldon. Want to go along?" said Robert with a slight fear she might say no.

"Sure. Sounds nice," she smiled.

*   *   *

Following the service in Sheldon, Arvella quietly asked, "Why did you choose to preach that particular sermon tonight?"

It was one he'd done once before, in seminary class. It was about the five wise, and the five foolish virgins.

"Well . . . I got an A on it in class," he responded, with a somewhat defensive tone.

"Now that's one sermon out of left field," she said, with a smile, slightly wrinkling her nose, "I don't think you'll want to preach it again."

"Do I respect her? Do I trust her?" Robert asked himself, later. "Boy, *do* I."

He sat down to write a letter to a friend—a fraternity brother named Bill Miedema.

"Dear Bill: I've met the girl I'm going to marry. . . ."

For the next two years, Robert and Arvella courted through letters as he finished his college studies. Then one evening, as they sat parked in his car, looking out at a star-filled sky twinkling over an Iowa pasture, Robert pulled a ring from his pocket—one he'd saved the $180 it cost him, from his weekend job at Montgomery Ward's department store. He looked directly into those sincere green eyes.

"Arvella. You know I love you. Will you marry me?"

"Yes," she responded, throwing her arms around him.

Only later did they realize the godwink symmetry of their wedding date: the middle of the year: June; the middle of the month: the 15th; and the middle of the century: 1950.

When Robert Schuller lifted the veil and kissed his bride, he knew that his greatest prayer had been answered—the one that he had uttered, subsequent to his college professor's advice to "start with your head, and your heart will follow." The prayer: "Lord, please lead me to the woman I should marry."

On their wedding night they each gave the other the precious gift of virginity.

In the same manner that Arvella counseled Robert following his second public sermon—with wisdom and candor—she has been a powerful partner in the building of their church, the Crystal Cathedral, in Anaheim, California. For twenty years, she has personally overseen the television production of their weekly services to over one hundred million people around the globe.

Robert Schuller has often looked back with awe upon the extraordinary godwink that delayed him from starting his summer job by one week, thereby placing him at the little church in Newkirk, Iowa, where he was able to meet Arvella, his future wife.

What would have happened to his life . . . to his ministry . . . if that scheduling godwink had not occurred?

Would Robert's prayer have been answered just the same?

Would God have simply found another way to intersect the lives of Robert and Arvella for a perfect marriage?

"We have lived in love and work for the last half of the last century, of the second millenium," says Robert, "And I'm still madly in love with her!"

Appreciation—
another step to successful relationships

I imagine that if you were a mouse in a corner of the Schuller household, any day of the week you would hear Robert or Arvella expressing genuine appreciation for each other. I've heard him tell others, in front of her, how tremendously important she is in his life. And Arvella never fails to remind him of his good points, emphasizing how much she appreciates them.

In fact, take any couple in this book and I'll wager that neither person will let the sun set on any day without expressing and reexpressing heartfelt appreciation for something, even the very smallest thing, that the other has done.

A powerful tool

Prayer is a powerful tool to help you improve yourself, your life, your security, and to help you find perfect love.

If you accept the premise that there is indeed someone up there who is bigger than all of us—someone who has created a destiny for you and placed you in a world surrounded by His perfection, from the changing of seasons to the birth of a new child; someone who nonetheless has given you the free will to accept or reject Him—why wouldn't this someone also be willing to listen, and reply to, your concerns and desires?

As you will see in story after story in this book, people who have wonderful soul mate relationships, also have a strong relationship with God. And they speak with Him every day, through prayer.

There is no right or wrong way to pray. It's just a conversation with you and your celestial father. But it is essential to have faith that your prayers are being heard and will be answered.

What is faith?

"Faith makes us sure of what we hope for and gives us proof of what we cannot see." So says the book of all answers, the Bible. If you have faith that your prayers will be answered, as Ray Materson's were even though he was locked behind prison walls, as Jess's were for Nicole's survival, as Robert Schuller's were to lead him to Arvella, they *will* be. It's as simple as that.

And what better way for God to communicate back to you, to let you know that He hears you, than to place a god-wink along your path?

Now, you have a word

The next time you have an answered prayer and you realize that there is no appropriate word in your vocabulary to *express* it—now you do.

You can say: "I just had a godwink."

4

The Power of Letting Go

Letting go is one of the hardest things to do.

It doesn't mean giving up.

It means that after you have done everything you possibly can to move yourself closer to the ideal of love and your perfect mate, you simply have to stop worrying about it and turn things over to the man upstairs.

Let go, and let God.

"Surrender to God and trust in His wisdom," I once heard my mentor, Dr. Norman Vincent Peale, say.

Still—because we like to control things, especially about our own lives—that's hard to do. We often try to pull God in the direction *we* want Him to go, forgetting that He's the guy who made the blueprint.

Sometimes we kid ourselves. We say we're "letting go," but

we keep our desires on a hidden tether, ready to pull them right back to our preoccupied minds.

Let go.

That's what you have to do.

There is a statement in the Scripture that says, "Having done all, stand." I must admit, I knew what the first part meant—to do all. But I was always unclear about the "standing" part.

From experience, I now know.

It means, once you've done all you reasonably can—let go. Turn the job over to the CEO in our lives, God, and let Him handle things from here on out.

As you will see from the stories I have collected for this chapter, Kimberly and Jerry, Tisha and Paul, and others, you can experience wonderful results when you let go.

First, I'd like to reprise a favorite love story from my initial book, *When God Winks*, featuring Alice and Jack. At the end, I'll bring you up to date on what has happened since their story was told.

Alice and Jack's remedy for love: let go

"If you want me to be married, Lord, *You* pick him out. So far my choices stink." Alice was looking skyward, with a look of finality.

With that, she dusted her hands up and down and surrendered the whole matter to God.

Failed relationships had been only one of the things getting her down. The latest doctor's report on her multiple sclerosis condition was also less than encouraging.

Throwing herself into her job and her part-time studies for a master's degree seemed to be the best antidote.

Not long after Alice let the matter of "men" drift from her mind, she succumbed to her sister's urgings to attend a social event.

"It'll do you some good just to get out," goaded her sister.

The event was pretty boring. She decided to leave early.

Stepping in front of a man near the exit, her eyes connected with his.

"They were the most beautiful golden-brown eyes I'd ever seen," sighed Alice.

The man introduced himself. His name was Jack.

"I think we shook hands for about three minutes," she now remembers with a smile.

They began talking. They talked and talked and talked. After nearly three hours—like Cinderella suddenly looking at her watch—Alice exclaimed: "Ohmygosh . . . I've got to go. I have to study for a test. And I'm going to my cousin's wedding this weekend . . . down in Victoria, Texas . . . and I'm not ready."

Jack looked at her.

"I'm *also* going to a wedding this weekend in Victoria," said Jack curiously, "My cousin's marrying a doctor."

"My cousin *is* a doctor!" shouted Alice.

Two people, who had just met, each going to a cousin's wedding, eight hours away—the *same* wedding. What are the odds of that?

Moreover, what do you *do* about it?

Save on gas.

They drove the five hundred miles to Victoria together, and there wasn't a moment of dead air—not a single loss for words.

At the wedding reception, Alice and Jack danced, again and again. "My feet hardly touched the floor," she remembers dreamily.

And when he kissed her good night, she said, "It made my toes curl."

The next morning Alice had breakfast with her favorite uncle, Charlie, and couldn't wait to tell him what was on her mind.

"I met the man I'm going to marry," she told Uncle Charlie.

"Does he know it?"

"No. But, he's the one. His name is Jack Totah."

"Jack Totah? I wonder if he's related to Nabe Totah?" asked Uncle Charlie.

Just then Jack entered the room.

"Yes, he's my uncle . . . out in California," said Jack.

"You won't believe this," said Uncle Charlie, slowly shaking his head, "But fifty years ago, I was on a boat coming to America, filled with uncertainty. I worried what would happen when I landed in this strange new land. Then, I met a young man who felt the same as me. Nabe Totah. We became the closest of friends, all across the ocean. When we got to customs . . . we were separated . . . and . . . I never saw my buddy Nabe again. I always wondered what happened to him. . . ."

As they listened, Alice and Jack looked at each other in disbelief.

This was just another in a powerful combination of godwinks that seemed to be sending them a confirming message that they were meant for each other.

One other matter did weigh on Alice's mind when she returned home, however. She worried that perhaps when Jack learned about her multiple sclerosis, his feelings might change for her.

"Maybe you shouldn't tell him," counseled one friend.

"No . . . I have to," said Alice.

When she mustered the courage to tell him, Jack looked at her—then looked down. A moment later he lifted his head to look her in the eyes, "I'm so sorry. What can I do to help you?" he asked.

Jack's response was more than she could have hoped for.

A year later . . . there was another wonderful wedding.

Alice and Jack's.

One of the most treasured snapshots in Alice's memory was when Jack lifted her veil to kiss her, he whispered, "I love you, forever."

Her heart melted all over again.

Another cherished snapshot was seeing Uncle Charlie and Uncle Nabe toasting the bride and groom, standing side by side, reunited after fifty years.

"I found my true soul mate and Uncle Charlie found his friend," said Alice. "Thank God. I mean *really* thank God!"

It all began when she surrendered.

It is indeed amazing what happens when we "let go" in the pursuit of a perfect mate. When we have the courage to do that, we are generally surprised with the results—sometimes guiding us to outcomes that we could never have imagined for ourselves.

Today, four years after I first wrote about Alice and Jack, they continue to grow their love for each other, with God, and with life. Add to that, a little boy, Jacob.

Alice struggles with the debilitating effects of multiple sclerosis, and has accepted the concept that the blessing of having one child can be "just enough."

Alice and Jack miss Uncle Nabe—who passed away—but see Uncle Charlie with some frequency, if he isn't fishing.

Kimberly, Kimberly—everywhere!

"I want a divorce!"

Jerry hung his head in disbelief. Kimberly, his wife of nine years, could have hit him over the head with a sledgehammer when that statement landed on him, out of the blue.

Certainly every couple has a few issues. Jerry had taken the initiative to schedule some counseling sessions with the pastor to straighten things out, but the first time the pastor forgot to show up. The second time Kimberly wouldn't go.

Now this.

Rejection felt like being tossed into the trash by somebody who didn't want you anymore.

He moved out right away thinking she just needed some space. And making things worse, she kept his hopes alive by bringing over his junk mail, making him think that maybe, just maybe, things would turn around.

He delayed signing the divorce papers as long as possible, then the lawyers told him they were going to drag him into court if he didn't sign.

Reluctantly, he signed.

For several months after his breakup with Kimberly, Jerry didn't date. Then, he started. And believe it or not, the girl he was attracted to was also named Kimberly.

They dated for eight or nine months. The relationship was "okay," but Jerry had the feeling that a good relationship was supposed to get better and better; instead, they just seemed to be drifting.

"Where is this headed?" Jerry kept wondering.

He decided to pray about it.

"Lord, what's the deal? Is this a name thing? Are you telling me the name *Kimberly* has anything to do with my failure in finding my soul mate?"

That day Jerry decided to drive over to see his sister in Biloxi, Mississippi, a three-hour drive from his home in the Florida panhandle. And yes—it *did* occur to him that there was something odd about this: his sister's name was *also* Kimberly.

Heading out of town, he stopped to pick up laundry. His *former wife* Kimberly was just leaving the cleaners. They had a few pleasantries and she went on her way. Then, before he could get away, his *girlfriend* Kimberly spotted his truck in the parking lot and she stopped to chat.

Anxious to get going to Biloxi, Jerry said his good-byes, and made his next stop—Kmart to pick up film. As he stood in line, the cashier was trying to get the attention of someone named Alice behind him. He turned and said to the lady, "I think she's talking to you."

"No, my name's Kimberly," she said.

Jerry blinked.

His next stop was the gas station. He went in to pay for the gas. He spotted the attendant's name tag—that's right—it was Kimberly.

Egads!

Five Kimberlys in the space of a half hour!

"Okay, Lord, thanks for the comedy," he muttered as he got on the interstate to Biloxi. It then occurred to him that, in a way, perhaps his prayer *was* being answered. That Kimberly *was* just a name; he should come to no conclusions about it, one way or the other.

Over the next few weeks Jerry continued to wonder if he would ever find a soul mate. Even if he tripped over her, how would he know she was the one?

Or, maybe his expectations were too high. Maybe there was something about himself that *he* didn't see, something that made him less desirable to the girl of his dreams.

"Then it struck me," he said, "I needed to give up trying to find her. I said, 'When you're ready, Lord, bring her to me.' "

That was that.

Soon he began to see the benefits of letting go.

"From that point on I was relieved. I was able to concentrate more at work. I felt at peace."

That's when Jerry got another surprise.

"My future wife showed up," he said, shaking his head, "And, you won't believe it—her name is Kimberly."

Kimberly Strickland was known as "Kiki" to her friends and family in Daytona Beach, Florida. She had achieved her college degree in Engineering Technology, a more hands-on, less cerebral section of the engineering world. In fact, to help her get into her chosen vocation, she purposely sought out her first job: that of a welder. Ignoring the looks of male coworkers, stunned by the incongruity of a beautiful woman pulling down her protective shield and picking up a blowtorch, she learned her trade from the ground up.

When it came time for Kiki to seriously seek career opportunities, she decided it was more professional-sounding to use her given name, Kimberly. So, that's the name she used on the résumés sent to headhunters and employment search firms.

One of her responses was from Alliance Laundry Systems in Panama City, Florida. Prior to speaking with the gentleman on the phone, she checked out the company on the internet. She was impressed. But . . . she had *no* interest in taking a job in the Florida panhandle.

When the man called, he was persuasive, and offered her a plane ticket to fly to Panama City for a face-to-face interview.

"I agreed to go, but secretly felt bad about it, knowing I didn't want the job," she said.

The people from Alliance Laundry Systems couldn't have been nicer. She liked them. She liked the company. She even liked the area. And when they sent her a letter offering more money and benefits than she had anticipated, she took the job.

Kimberly didn't know it at the time, but she was making a decision that would affect her life in more ways than one.

"The first time I saw Jerry, I was walking through the plant on my initial tour," recalls Kimberly. "Stepping over sheet metal, and dodging obstacles, I couldn't take my eyes off of him. I guess it was his confident persona as he spoke with a group of his workers."

When Kimberly checked in to the nurse's office to fill out health-care forms, Jerry popped his head in to ask the nurse a question. "Who is he?" she whispered, when he departed.

"That's Jerry Fry. He's the sweetest guy," said the nurse.

Later, someone introduced them, and Kimberly felt a tingling deep inside.

Several days passed.

"Have you thought of asking out that new engineer?" a coworker asked Jerry. It was the third time he'd mentioned it.

"She wouldn't be interested in me," he said. "She's a college grad. I'm a laborer. I'm not her caliber."

"You're wrong," said the friend, "She mentioned something about you."

"Really?"

A short while later, Kimberly initiated a conversation.

"What are you doing after work?"

"Just going out to the creek—goin' for a swim," said Jerry.

"Hey, that's a good idea. Mind if I follow you there in my car?"

Seeing her behind the wheel of her car in his rearview mirror, Jerry thought, "Boy, she really is beautiful." Glancing skyward, in a low voice, he said, "Guide me, Lord. Don't let me make any mistakes."

Walking on the sandbar in the middle of the creek, Jerry decided he'd better get something off his chest right at the outset. He told her about all the Kimberlys. He wanted to see if it scared her off.

She was amused. Not at all scared.

When she left, Jerry resumed his private conversation with the Man above. "How will I know if she's the one?" he asked. Then added, "I hope she is."

She was.

And *he* was the one for Kimberly.

It didn't take either of them very long to know it, either. But Kimberly had some resistance from home.

"What???" was the startled response from Kimberly's mother, "You've only known him for two months? You can't get married this soon!" pleaded her mother, "You need time to get to know each other."

Yet, Kimberly was resolved. When Jerry had asked her to marry him, she knew he was the one. And there was no sense waiting. However, when they called the courthouse about getting a marriage license, they found that Florida had a mandatory four-day waiting period. That meant they had to wait until the following Monday to get married, September 20, the same day Kimberly was scheduled to close on a house. So that's what they did; they went to the bank for the closing that morning, and got married in the afternoon.

For weeks Kimberly's mother continued to fret about her daughter's snap judgment to commit herself to matrimony after knowing Jerry for only a few weeks.

Then one day her mother ran into some friends that she and Kimberly had once visited after church. The Bohannons. She recalled that day that she and her daughter had both enjoyed looking at photos of the couple's fiftieth wedding anniversary. But it was something Kimberly's mother remembered the couple saying that afternoon, that caused a softening of her heart toward her daughter's short engagement.

"My mother called me and said she'd seen the Bohannons," said Kimberly. "We talked about how surprised we had been the day they were showing us their photos and they told us that they got married *after knowing each other for only two weeks!* I reminded my Mother that Jerry and I had known each other *four times* as long as that! Eight weeks!

But what really sealed it was when my mom excitedly said, "Kimberly, you won't believe this: you and the Bohannons share the same anniversary date! September twentieth!"

"Can you imagine?" Kimberly continued. "The Bohannons got married after only two weeks and *their* marriage lasted more than fifty years. And—just because of that silly Florida law making us wait four days—we were married on their anniversary, September twentieth."

It was a godwink of reassurance—for Kimberly's mother, to be sure, but also for for Kimberly and Jerry. They have been happily married for five years.

They have also been blessed with the birth of a baby boy, notwithstanding their worry when he was diagnosed with a rare childhood illness. Kimberly was torn about going back to work after her maternity leave. She was concerned about leaving her baby with child care.

Now she and Jerry have come to a prayerful decision: Jerry has always loved children, and he has elected to leave his job to be the stay-at-home parent, while Kimberly continues her engineering career.

With the wider perspective of hindsight, Kimberly and Jerry look to the past with a thankful heart. Jerry, in particular, can now clearly see the merits of sometimes coming to that place in life where you need to simply let go, and let God; to surrender all your worries about a particular problem, and really believe that things are going to turn out all right.

Meanwhile, Kimberly and Jerry look to their future with a strong faith. The many godwinks in their past—including the multiple Kimberlys and the coincidence of their wedding day being the same as old friends'—provide them with a feeling of certainty that godwinks will continue to unfold into their future.

What can we learn from their story? That having the faith to let go—to surrender the way Jerry did, putting your mind on matters other than searching for a mate—can pay off for you, the way it did for him and Kimberly.

Another message— another step to success in relationships

There is another message I hope you will take away from Kimberly and Jerry's story, as well as Alice and Jack's. A message of support.

We all have the need to have someone we can rely on.

Someone we can trust who will be watching our backs. To catch us if we fall. To provide a shoulder to cry on. We need to know that our partner is there to support us. Never to tear us down—especially in front of others—but to build us up. To give us constant messages of support.

When Jack said to Alice, upon learning that she had MS, "What can I do to help?" he was demonstrating support. When Jerry volunteered to quit his job to become the stay-at-home father of their child who was in fragile health, so that Kimberly could maintain her higher-level job with peace of mind, he was her system of support.

Back to the principle of letting go. In the next scenario, both parties let go.

Tisha and Paul: at my most beautiful

Tisha and Paul both had troubling relationships.

Tisha had a five-year relationship that wasn't going anywhere.

Paul had several dead-end relationships.

They both attended Lubbock Christian University. Tisha a junior. Paul a senior.

Paul was not the kind of guy Tisha would have normally gone for. Tisha was not the kind of girl Paul had dated.

They both did something at the same time: they both

surrendered—both purposely turned to prayer and said, "I give it up. I leave it for you, God, to bring me the person I am to marry."

The first time they met, Tisha was in the school cafeteria with a girlfriend.

Paul was not normally in the cafeteria at that time. He liked avoiding peak traffic time. But that evening he had an obligation and, carrying his tray, he looked around. There was only one seat available—across from Tisha.

"What struck me was how much I laughed," said Tisha. "We had this conversation and everything he said made me laugh."

They talked.

And talked, and talked. Their first phone conversation, the next night, lasted five hours.

"I knew in that conversation that Paul was the person I was going to marry," confesses Tisha.

"Me too," said Paul.

"But the feelings were so strong that I just wanted to run away from them, then everywhere I turned, the name 'Paul' just kept popping up: in conversations, in things I read . . . everywhere! It seemed like a confirmation that I *wasn't* supposed to run away."

"There was this song I played for Tisha," said Paul. "It wasn't a top-forty hit or anything like that, but everywhere we went, that song was playing. On elevators, at the mall, on a car radio as we were walking by. It was an REM song, 'At My Most Beautiful.' "

"That song came on every time I started questioning my feelings," said Tisha.

After only a few months, sitting in Tisha's dorm, Paul formally asked the question that seemed to naturally emerge from their conversations: "Tisha . . . will you marry me?"

Nine months after they met, they were married.

Everything fell into place, said Tisha. "When I went to my mother to tell her we were getting married I was worrying about how we could have a wedding and afford to find a place to live. But she surprised me with something I didn't know: for years my grandfather had put away money for my wedding. So, we not only had the money to get started, but we had a honeymoon at Disney World."

Tisha and Paul are happily married, with a two-year-old daughter. She's a teacher; he's in advertising.

What do they say are the three most important things for a successful relationship?

Tisha: trust, love, and forgiveness.

Paul: communication, trust, and humor.

Go ahead—try it. Let go.

Do you think you could do what Alice Totah did? To say, "If you want me to be married, Lord, *You* pick him out. So far my choices stink"?

Can you muster the same faith Jerry Fry had when he said, "When you're ready, Lord, bring her to me"?

Could you follow the example of Tisha and Paul, who individually said, "I give it up. I leave it to you, God, to bring me the person I am to marry"?

Shortly after their surrender, each was rewarded with an opening of pathways directly to their soul mates.

Go ahead, try it. Let go.

Let go, but test your feelings

When you let go, you no longer perseverate that you haven't yet found your ideal mate. You instead put your desires out there, out of mind, and wait for the perfect circumstances to appear.

How will you know?

Test yourself. When you do meet someone and strong feelings come over you, ask if this is really love, or just infatuation. Is this the real thing, or your desire to *be* in love?

I recently overheard my wife reminding our daughter that infatuation is like buying a pair of shoes. You sometimes see a pair of shoes that you "just have to have." They're the perfect color. The heel is just right. They look like a million bucks on your feet. But . . . they're just a little narrow in the toe. The saleslady says the leather will stretch. You accept what she says because you're otherwise really infatuated with those shoes. You *want* them to fit. You buy them.

It doesn't take long. By the end of the evening you know that you've made a very painful mistake. Your infatuation pushed you into a false belief that you had a perfect fit.

It wasn't.

5

Godwink Links

It has happened to all of us. We bump into someone we never expected to meet, and they in turn are responsible for leading us onto a whole new path in life.

Sometimes we are led to a new job, new customers, new friends—experiences that never would have happened if that particular person had not come along at that very moment.

Isn't that exactly how most people are introduced to love in life? Someone "just happens" along and becomes the connecting element between two people; a relationship is nurtured, they fall in love, and eventually find themselves walking down the aisle.

You can probably think of many times in your own life where, had it not been for that "chance" meeting with that *very* person at that *very* moment, your life would have gone into a distinctly different direction.

You may even conclude that those encounters were god-winks.

But rather than looking at those experiences from *your* perspective and outcome, I want you to focus on *the person who just "happened" to come your way*. What caused *them* to be there at that very instant? To become radically involved in the direction of your life at that precise point in time?

Is it possible that they were divinely directed?

Is it possible that without their consciously knowing it, they were unwitting messengers of godwinks to you?

I believe that we are *all* unwitting messengers at one time or another—what I call "Godwink Links"—in the lives of others; emissaries of joy, rarely realizing what a wonderful role we are fulfilling.

My book: an unwitting messenger

Since writing *When God Winks*, my original book in this series, I have enjoyed receiving many emails and notes from readers who said that the book itself became a Godwink Link in their lives.

A nurse in Minnesota, Priscilla Kilibarda, wrote how my book almost became an animated object as she contemplated buying it, then attempted to put it back on the bookstore shelf, and how it refused to go back into the space from which it came, and when she laid it on a table and began to walk away, the book thudded to the floor.

She bought it.

But when she opened the book randomly to a chapter about godwinks and a life-saving love story, she was startled. It was about Dr. Louis Graber, the father of the doctor for whom she worked.

She began reading.

Years before, as he was leaving a medical conference in Milwaukee, Dr. Graber wrestled with whether he should take in one last lecture for a highly unusual medical procedure. If he did, he might not get back home to Oshkosh at the appointed time.

Meanwhile, in Oshkosh a young man named Eric Fellman was working on a summer job driving heavy railroad equipment, and thinking about his impending marriage to his college sweetheart, Joy.

The machine stopped running.

Eric climbed down to look beneath the two-ton machine to see if it was something he could fix. But he'd forgotten to set the brake.

The apparatus began to move!

Lights flashed in his head!

He tasted warm blood as the heavy steel rollers crushed him!

With incredible fortuity, Eric was *not* in the middle of nowhere, where most of his time was spent, on miles of lonely Midwest railroad tracks; the accident occurred at a railroad crossing. Someone spotted that Eric was in trouble, and called for help.

Doctors in the Oshkosh hospital quickly assessed that he had massive loss of blood; his vital signs were dropping, and worried that the next worst thing might happen—a burst liver. For that organ, like a sponge, is very difficult to repair with sutures. Loss of life often accompanies that kind of tragedy.

Then, the worst thing *did* happen! His liver burst.

But Eric Fellman was about to receive a remarkable god-wink!

Just as Eric was entering surgery, Dr. Louis Graber was returning from the medical conference. He knew exactly what to do! Skillfully he lifted the membrane from the sides of the liver, folded them on top, clamped them, and the bleeding stopped.

His knowledge of this new procedure to mend a ruptured liver was learned by *taking in that last lecture* in Milwaukee.

Eric was saved.

And, though slightly delayed, so was his wedding to Joy.

Today, Eric and Joy Fellman are living happily ever after,

and have committed themselves to a ministry involved with U.S. congressmen.

Surprised to read this story in a book that had seemed to demand her attention, Nurse Kilibarda immediately informed her boss, and he promptly called his father.

Dr. Graber remembered the case and couldn't believe that his story was in a book. Of late, he had been in low spirits with the loss of his dear wife. But, in a way, this godwink experience—being reminded of a young couple's love story that had lived because he had once unwittingly taken in a last lecture—was like a divine gift, making him feel more connected to his own recently lost love.

"Who knows," wrote Nurse Kilibarda. "Maybe all Dr. Graber needed was a little sign from an angel above to know that he too was an angel in someone else's life."

Dr. Louis Graber had once become the Godwink Link in the life of Eric Fellman. Now, in the end, it was my little book—almost chasing after the nurse—that represented the Godwink Link that was oblivious to its mission of hope in the lives of others.

We never know . . .

Come to think of it, I suspect none of us can recall a time when we actually *knew* that we were being directed to be a

Godwink Link in someone else's life. With the attention always on the outcome, and never on the unwitting *messenger*, it is easy for our roles in the delivery of a godwink to become totally obscured.

This is apparent in the following stories. Your attention will be naturally drawn to the outcome, but try to force yourself to identify the Godwink Links, the unwitting players who help each story unfold to its conclusion.

Brigitta, Marco, and Mother Teresa

"That's the best news I've had all day!" said Marco.

The flight attendant just offered him a free upgrade to first class on his flight from Bombay, India to London. He was being rewarded as a frequent flyer on that route.

The amenities of first class travel—the food, the wine, and the additional legroom were welcomed on a long flight—not to mention the convenience of being in the front of the plane when it was time to get off.

Marco, tall, handsome, and Italian, placed his carry-on bags into the overhead compartment and slipped into the wide leather seat.

"Hummm . . . there's *another* benefit," he thought, looking at the attractive blonde he would be seated next to. He smiled at her. She smiled back.

Pulling out his London *Times*, he studied the headlines and then checked the weather forecast. Foggy.

"Well, it looks like we will have a foggy day in London-town," he said to the lady, parodying an old song.

"That's typical, isn't it," she rejoined, in a sweet German accent.

Now that Marco had achieved eye contact and the seedlings of a conversation, he ventured further. "Are you traveling to London for work or pleasure?"

"I'm connecting there to Berlin. I frequently travel from Berlin to Bombay on business," she said.

"What do you do?"

"I work for a German chemical manufacturer. My assigned territory is India."

"Really. I also travel to India frequently. I'm part of an international medical research team. My name's Dr. Marco Iannuzzi," he said.

"How do you do. My name is Brigitta."

During the long flight Marco and Brigitta chatted easily. Their backgrounds—his medical, hers chemical—provided many common denominators. When their conversation moved to the beneficiaries of their work—families suffering from disease and hunger—Mother Teresa's legendary work with the poor, first in Calcutta, then in many places around the world, became the center of their attention.

"I met her once," offered Marco proudly, knowing that it was an extraordinary badge of honor to have been in the presence of an international icon.

"So did I!" said Brigitta with equal enthusiasm.

"Really?" reacted Marco. "That's incredible . . . two people seated next to each other by happenstance, both having met Mother Teresa, in person. Tell me how you met her."

"It was in Bombay . . ." began Brigitta, describing the situation, then asking: "How did you meet Mother Teresa?"

Marco explained that his good fortune occurred when Mother Teresa was in Rome, several years earlier, visiting her nuns near the Vatican.

For the balance of the flight Marco and Brigitta talked endlessly. They learned they were both unmarried. And that both devoted so much time to their work that little time was available for developing relationships.

The flight arrived in London.

"It was very nice meeting you," said Marco, smiling as he stood to leave the plane.

"Yes. I enjoyed our chat," smiled Brigitta.

They went their separate ways.

It occurred to each that they had just been with someone they really liked, with whom they had much in common. Would they ever see each other again?

"I didn't even get her phone number," Marco scolded himself as he rushed to his connecting flight.

"I don't even know where he lives," said Brigitta to herself.

*   *   *

It was two years later. Rome.

That was home base for Marco. He was scheduled to entertain several friends at a favorite restaurant that was quite suitable for large parties. When, at the last minute, two couples had to cancel, Marco decided to switch reservations to another favorite restaurant—one that was more cozy and intimate.

While handing his coat to the maître d' he accidentally bumped into someone. He turned to apologize. He was looking into the surprised eyes of Brigitta.

"Brigitta! What are you doing here in Rome?" he exclaimed with a wide smile.

"I'm here to shop and have three days of vacation." She smiled back.

"We must get together. Do you have lunch plans for tomorrow?"

"Not unless you ask me," she responded coyly.

The lunch, at a romantically charming restaurant, another of Marco's favorites, lasted three hours. Their conversation seemed to pick up right where they had left off two years earlier.

"Do you have time to take a walk, to let me show you some of the sights of my city?" charmed Marco.

For two hours they walked through narrow, cobblestone streets marveling at structures that dated to the earliest of times. Brigitta enjoyed Marco's enthusiasm for his city, and laughed easily at his flamboyant stories and descriptions.

By chance, while walking near the Vatican, they saw some nuns, who were with the order of Mother Teresa, entering a building. They inquired about Mother Teresa and were invited in to say prayers in the chapel.

It seemed fitting that Mother Teresa, who had been a significant factor in their initial conversation two years earlier, would play a prayerful role in their serendipitous meeting in Rome.

For two days Marco and Brigitta absorbed the sights, the shopping, and the restaurants of Rome, engaging in animated, nonstop conversation. Unstated, however, was the unlikelihood of their being able to get together again, given their careers and distant domiciles.

They hugged. They said good-bye.

Two more years passed.

Brigitta was delivered a frightening medical report. The lump she had found in her breast was of great concern because of her work in the chemical industry. Surgery was scheduled. As she worried about the impending uncertainties, Brigitta decided to write a letter to Mother Teresa, to ask for prayers. She had no idea who at Mother Teresa's convent would answer her—if anyone—but it gave her comfort to write.

What Brigitta did *not* know was that Mother Teresa had a firm policy: she personally answered every letter she received.

Brigitta stared at Mother Teresa's handwritten signature at the bottom of a neatly typed letter, personally promising prayers for a successful surgical procedure. Brigitta made a secret personal pact: if she lived and recovered, she would go to India and volunteer to work in Mother Teresa's homes for the sick and dying.

Two more years passed.

Marco was on a medical research trip to Calcutta, meeting with several doctors, one of whom offered to give him a lift back to his hotel. En route, the doctor said to Marco, "Do you mind if I make a stop on the way back? I have to check on a patient at the Woodlands Nursing Home."

"No. That would be fine," said Marco.

"Why don't you join me, Doctor," said the friend, smiling. "You might enjoy meeting my patient."

Donning white lab coats, the two doctors went down a hall and entered a room. There, in bed, recovering from cardiac difficulties, Marco was shocked to see Mother Teresa herself! They spent a few minutes, exchanged doctor-patient pleasantries with the world's most famous nun, then said their good-byes.

Emerging from the room, Marco was starting to tell the doctor what a surprise he had given him when, from the corner of his eye, he saw an approaching group of nuns, and one lady in civilian clothing.

It was Brigitta!

"Wha-what are you doing here!" exclaimed Marco.

Beaming with surprise and joy, Brigitta replied excitedly, "I'm doing volunteer work in Calcutta, and Mother Teresa's nuns have arranged for me to meet her . . . to thank her personally for praying for my successful recovery from an operation."

"You've been on my mind. I must see you!" said Marco.

"Yes—I've been thinking of you, too. Can you wait for me? While I see Mother?"

After a short meeting with Mother Teresa, Brigitta returned to the waiting arms of Marco. This time, they both knew that the powerful godwinks—repeatedly delivered by their Godwink Link, Mother Teresa—were heavenly magnets redundantly pulling the two soul mates together.

They never again left each other's embrace.

Marco and Brigitta were married in 1998, and thrive in the romantic ambience of their home in Rome.

Mother Teresa had no idea . . .

The person who brought me this story, Bradley James, is a man who knew Mother Teresa for eleven years. He's gifted musically, a marvelous pianist and composer, but his work with the missions of Mother Teresa came out of an inexplicable attraction to her from the time he was a boy. Through a wonderful godwink story in itself he came to meet her, work with her, and she subsequently allowed him to translate all of her writings to music.

I asked Bradley what she would have said if she had known she was the Godwink Link—the unawares catalyst—in the lives of Marco and Brigitta.

His reply was unhesitating.

"She would have said, 'We are all called to be a pencil in His hand—we just have to get out of the way.' "

The following story shows how God uses not only people, but other things to weave a Godwink Link between people in love.

The holiday tapestry

The storm clouds of winter dissipated over the village where Pastor Nance was preparing for his "grand opening," as he liked to call it. Christmas Eve—one day away—would inaugurate his assignment to the historic but woefully dilapidated church.

As the heavy doors creaked open, he was anxious to see the newly painted and plastered sanctuary that he and a group of volunteers had completed the evening before, just ahead of the storm.

He stood in the entryway, not in awe, but in utter shock. During the night a leak in the roof ripped a gaping hole in the wall right behind the pulpit.

"Oh no! Now what am I going to do?" he said, shaking his

head, quickly calculating that there was no way the damage could be repaired before the next day's festivities.

"I need a miracle, Lord," he declared aloud, rolling his eyes heavenward, as he slumped dejectedly toward his study in the back of the church.

Passing a pile of unsold items from the holiday bazaar, his eyes were drawn to something. Stepping closer, he lifted the edges of what appeared to be a huge tapestry—a finely woven tablecloth—oversize for any ordinary table.

An idea struck him! Yes! This huge tapestry could be just the thing he needed!

By day's end he'd completed his plan. Departing the church, the pastor turned, with a self-satisfied smile, to take one last look at the fruits of his "miracle."

The old tapestry was nailed to the wall and completely masked the nasty hole.

He'd almost reached his car when he realized that he'd absent-mindedly left his car keys on his desk. He returned to the church, passing the bus stop, where he spotted a small woman huddled in the cold.

"Hello? How long have you been waiting?" he asked.

Her dark eyes looked at him with uncertainty.

She shivered, and her voice was weak as she slowly spoke in broken English: "One hour."

"Come inside and get warm while I get my keys. I can drive you home," he offered.

When Pastor Nance returned from his study he didn't see the old woman.

Then he found her—she was standing behind the pulpit examining the tapestry in the dim light of the church. Her wrinkled fingers stroked it fondly.

"This is mine," she whispered.

"Yours?"

"Yes. Those are my initials," she said, pointing to the corner of the tapestry.

Responding to the confused look on his face, she continued, "In Austria we had a big table . . . I wove this with my own hands. In the war I lost my home . . . I was separated from my husband . . ." her voice trailed as tears glistened in her eyes, ". . . and never saw him again."

In disbelief the pastor stammered, "You . . . must take this with you," reaching for the tapestry.

"No," she forbade, raising her hand in a halting gesture. "You keep it here. I have no place for it."

It was a quiet ride though the darkened streets. The pastor was nearly speechless as he said good-bye and watched her lonely form disappear into her modest dwelling.

All the way home, he pondered the powerful significance of what he had witnessed. What are the odds, he thought, that this woman, at a lonely bus stop, would somehow be connected to a tapestry that he had just hung inside the old church?

And what an incredible godwink for this extraordinary experience to occur at such a critical turning point in his own life—the commencement of his new ministry. It was truly mind-boggling!

The next evening arrived with all the hustle and bustle of an expectant holiday. Children costumed as small sheep and shepherds scurried to rehearsed places, as a miniature Mary gently cradled a baby doll. Candlelight flickered across Rubenesque faces, and the old church came alive with joyful caroling.

Pastor Nance swelled with satisfaction. His "grand opening" was a success.

At the end of the evening, when the last hand was shook, and the last Merry Christmas wished, he felt a wonderful sense of peace. Everyone gone, he turned to look, just one more time, at the miracle tapestry that now seemed to be right at home behind the pulpit.

But something—a ghostly figure near the tapestry—caused his eyes to narrow!

"Hello?" he asked into the dim light.

No answer.

"Hello?" he repeated, hesitantly stepping closer.

No answer.

"Oh . . ." he sighed, "it's you, Hans," relieved that it was only the church's clock repairman.

Hans was staring at the tapestry.

"Is everything all right, Hans?"

"This is mine," he answered tentatively, with a Viennese inflection.

"I beg your pardon?"

"This is mine. My wife made this for our home in Austria. Those are her initials. It was with our belongings . . . in the war . . . when we lost each other."

His eyes moistened.

But Pastor Nance was well ahead of him. Tears had already begun to glisten on his cheeks as the cascading godwinks revealed the *real* miracle. The tapestry was not just a solution for a damaged church wall, it was—along with the pastor himself—the Godwink Link between two lost soul mates.

"Hans . . . would you come with me, please?" asked Pastor Nance. "I want to drive you somewhere . . . for the best holiday gift you've ever received."

It is hard to imagine the extraordinary joy Pastor Nance carried with him for the rest of his days on earth—the image of himself standing next to the bewildered Hans, at the door of a strange house; the anticipation he must have felt, waiting for the door to open, and to witness the joy in those two faces—Hans and his long lost love—ignited by the light of God's love.

Pastor Nance felt forever blessed—*richly* blessed—to have been an unwitting messenger in the lives of these two forlorn souls.

Threads in the fabric of life

Godwinks are ubiquitously woven into the fabric of our lives, each a tapestry of many colors—sad and happy—and they are often interlaced by unexpected emissaries of joy: Godwink Links.

Take a few moments right now. Reflect upon your own experiences over the past few days and weeks. Was there someone for whom you provided a Godwink Link? Were you the unwitting emissary of joy to someone through a phone call or an introduction?

Think back to when you played "connect the dots" in a picture book as a kid. If you "connect the dots" with people you have encountered whose lives have been changed as a result, you'll be surprised. The emerging picture will show an endless connection between you and the lives of others. You may have been the reason someone connected with a new career, a new spiritual awakening, or new love in their life. You were a Godwink Link.

The man or woman who fulfills your every desire for a deep, lasting love may also arrive into your midst through a Godwink Link.

Look around you. Perhaps someone who is unknowingly being employed as an angel on earth is already in your presence.

6

Expecting the Unexpected

As I think about the point I want to make to you in this chapter, my mind drifts to a popular TV series a few years back: *Candid Camera*.

The show regularly delivered on its promise of unexpectedly "catching people in the act of being themselves," as unsuspecting participants were filmed in silly situations cooked up by the producers.

No one was safe.

Each of us was the potential prey of snooping, lurking cameras—according to the theme song that ended every program: "When you least expect it . . . smile . . . you're on *Candid Camera*," the song ended with gusto.

That's sometimes the way it is in real life. The love that you have long desired, the person you seemed to be preordained to spend the rest of your life with, just pops up "when you least expect it."

More often than not, godwinks are unexpected little signals to you that bolster your spirits. And the more you see them, the more they occur. If, over a month or so, you write down every godwink that happens to you—small and large—you will be astonished at how long the list turns out to be.

I therefore urge you to expect the unexpected godwinks that I *know* are going to unfold in your life. Expect them, and enjoy them. And when they happen, smile—because you'll know you're up there on someone's "candid camera."

Following are three wonderfully distinct stories about people who received the joy of unexpected godwinks.

Jhannea and Chad—
Mr. Postman, send me a dream

It was an exciting yet daring time for Jhannea Frandsen. She had finished graduate studies in audiology at Arizona State University and learned about a job opportunity in Grand Forks, North Dakota. Although that was twenty-six hours from where she grew up in Arizona, she applied for the job, and got it.

She found a nice apartment—number 15, at 2024 30th Avenue South.

Having just moved, she knew no one. She had no girl-friends. And as for men, they seldom had been much of a fac-tor for Jhannea. She'd never dated anyone seriously.

Although—truth be known—she *had* noticed a man in the building, but . . . he looked younger than she was.

Chad Ringenberg looked young for his age. He lived in apart-ment number 16, at 2024 30th Avenue South. He was drawn to Grand Forks by his work in the use of Global Positioning Systems to improve agricultural production. Chad was not in-volved with anyone and he'd had no serious relationships for three years.

Had he noticed that pretty blonde who lived in his build-ing? Yes, he'd seen her sitting on her second floor patio. He *did* wonder about her. She looked nice. But . . . Chad was not the type to just go up and start a conversation.

"How *could* I meet her?" he ruminated, walking past her patio, looking at her through a squinted eye.

Then, Chad had a godwink he could never have expected. A Godwink Link, in fact. The mailman. His name was Dave Guzeman.

It was a good job for Dave Guzeman. He'd worked the same route for thirteen years, there were nice benefits, and thanks to rotation schedules, he had a Saturday off every six weeks.

In over two decades with the postal service he was proud

that, as far as he knew, he had never misdelivered a single letter. Not until this one time.

Chad came home from work and opened his mailbox. The power company bill addressed to Jhannea Frandsen, his next-door neighbor, had been delivered to him by mistake.

"What an unexpected opportunity," he thought, "This is my chance to meet her!"

For two hours he waited.

"Maybe she's having dinner," he calculated, "Maybe around seven would be a good time."

At seven o'clock Chad went out the door, around the corner, paused a long moment, and took a deep breath before knocking.

She opened the door.

"Her eyes lit up when I introduced myself," said Chad, "And told her I had her power bill."

Conversation was remarkably easy. They began chatting, drifting from one topic to the next, and stood talking in the doorway for two hours. Finally, they looked at their watches, and mutually said, "Well, see you around."

The next day, by good fortune, was a day off—the second Saturday in September. Chad had been thinking about Jhannea ever since he had left her front door, and by the middle of the next morning, he was again knocking on her door, asking if she would like to have dinner and a movie later.

Yes, she would.

The courtship of Jhannea and Chad began. For the next twenty months they dated, getting to know each other. They not only had similar personalities but compatible interests, as well. Jhannea came from a family of strong Christian beliefs. Chad was raised as a Catholic. Together they came to an understanding that building a bond of faith was to be the number one factor in their relationship.

They began talking so casually about marriage that matrimony eventually seemed almost inevitable. And when Chad one day said, "Let's take a walk in the park," Jhannea was suspicious. As he moved them down a walkway toward a monument, Jhannea spotted several people hanging out there and it instantly occurred to her that, if a proposal was on Chad's mind, she surely didn't want to have such a special moment played out in front of an audience.

"Let's go back to the apartment," said Jhannea, rapidly.

There, steps from where they had first stood in the doorway in a two-hour conversation, Chad looked into Jhannea's eyes, and asked, "Will you marry me?"

Throwing her arms around him, she whispered, "Yes."

Wedding planning did not need to be a long process, in their view. When they telephoned the church to find an open date over the next three or four months, they felt fortunate: one Saturday was available. The second Saturday in September.

It did not occur to Jhannea and Chad until some time later that they were experiencing another godwink. They were to be married on *the same weekend, exactly two years after they had met.*

It *did* occur to them, however, that without the god-wink of postman Dave Guzeman's misdelivered power bill, they might never have gotten together.

"We should invite the mailman," said Jhannea jokingly one day, in front of her parents.

"What a great idea," said her dad.

So when Jhannea went to the Grand Forks post office to mail her wedding invitations, she had an extra one addressed to, "The postman for 2024 30th Avenue South." She asked the supervisor if he would see that it was given to the proper person.

Dave Guzeman thought it odd that his supervisor would hand him a wedding invitation. He took it home and threw it on the bureau. He never gave it another thought until one day he was stopped by a couple driving along his route.

"Are you the mailman for these apartments?" asked Jhannea's father.

Dave nodded.

"Did you get your invitation?"

He was puzzled.

"The invitation to my daughter's wedding . . . we hope you'll be coming."

When Dave got back home that night he picked up the invitation. "What do ya know," he thought. "That Saturday is the only Saturday I have off in six weeks."

Dave was surprised when he got to the church. As people filed in, there was a huge mailbox in the vestibule for them to place congratulatory cards into. An usher spotted Dave, greeted him as if he were a special guest, and took him right down to one of the front rows.

Later, when Dave saw video footage of the wedding he saw the surprised look on his own face: he was coincidentally framed in the picture just as the minister began the wedding ceremony by holding up and talking about the power bill that was Dave's only goof in twenty-three years on the job.

"Without that misdirected power bill, surely by a divine power," said the pastor, "this wedding might never have happened."

As the newly married couple turned to walk down the aisle, they were center stage in a virtual sea of smiling faces, as the music of the Beatles resonated in the background: "Oh yes . . . wait a minute Mr. Postman . . ."

The next day, a cute story about the postman theme of Jhannea and Chad's wedding turned up in the local paper and was subsequently picked up by the Associated Press. For weeks friends reported from around the country that they'd heard about their wedding on the radio. Then, *Good Morning America* got drift of it, and flew them into New York for an interview, along with Dave the postman. The story of their marvelous godwinks went coast to coast.

One year after they were married, I asked Jhannea to name the three most important factors in her relationship with Chad. In reverse order she said:

"Third, working together through difficulties.

"Second, to love each other unconditionally.

"First and foremost: faith," she said with an emphasis on "faith," before continuing. "To establish a relationship with Jesus Christ, and to be committed to that, no matter what."

One wonders if Jhannea and Chad ever drew a connection between this, her primary point, and the initials on their wedding memorabilia: J–C.

When you add up the unexpected godwinks that happened to Jhannea and Chad, they seem to line up like lighthouse beacons, directing their actions.

- Chad and Jhannea rented adjacent apartments in the same building;
- The postman, Dave, misdelivered the mail for the first time;
- The wedding fell on Dave's only Saturday off in six weeks;
- They were married on the same weekend they had met, two years earlier.

Expecting the unexpected takes faith

When you put your mind in a place where you are open to receiving unexpected godwinks, you are really stepping out in faith. Believing that godwinks *will* happen to you—just the way you count on those signs being there on the highways, or on street corners to guide you along—is an important step to *receiving* them.

As with Chad and Jhannea, your unexpected godwinks can be expected, even if they are really unbelievable, as in the story that follows.

Clair Miller's unbelievably unexpected Godwinks

One more American hamburger before shipping out for the cold uncertainties of World War II seemed like a good idea to Clair Miller, a twenty-nine-year old Air Force gunner. It was Christmas Eve, 1943.

"Let's go," he said to his seven crewmates, salivating at the thought that this might be his last hamburger for many months. The war was raging in Europe, and he was bound from March Field in California to somewhere in England. It was sure to be dangerous.

As one of the oldest crew members, Miller had an almost paternal relationship with the rest of them. His natural leadership and altruism—always counseling the younger airmen—led them to nickname him "Dad."

At the local diner a pretty waitress took their orders. As she overheard the boisterous conversations (probably disguising their nervousness) she called for their attention.

"Hey, you guys. I have a boyfriend over there somewhere. How about taking him my picture!"

The crew all looked at Clair.

"Sure, let me have it," said Clair, not wishing to disappoint the young woman by telling her the impossibility of what she was asking. After all, it was Christmas Eve.

Eight months later in August 1944, Clair and his crew were in the thick of things. Their B-17 was taking heavy anti-aircraft fire in a flight over Holland when an explosion preceded the pilot's orders for everyone to bail out. The plane was going to blow up!

Clair's parachute dropped him to the ground. He looked around—none of his crew was with him. He looked for a way to escape, but within minutes enemy soldiers surrounded him and the next morning he found himself in the worst possible situation: facing a firing squad.

As he looked his captors in the eye, Clair called deeply upon his faith. Focusing on the intent faces that were staring back at him, through the crosshairs of rifles, he said a prayer and smiled, satisfied that he'd turned this impossible situation over the only one who could deal with the impossible.

At that moment three women ran toward the firing squad shouting, "He's a Yank, not a Brit!"

Why would that make a difference? The Americans were the enemy of German soldiers just as the British were. But, for some unknown reason, the firing squad lowered their rifles, and Clair was saved.

Clair was subsequently shuttled into a crowded train car and transported to several unknown destinations before ending up at a prisoner of war camp called Stalag Luft IV behind German lines in eastern Prussia, part of what is now Poland. There, some 10,000 prisoners of war were held captive.

As was his nature, Clair worried less about himself than about those around him. Again others turned to him for counsel and encouragement; they trusted this "older" American airman who seemed so secure in his faith and values.

The days passed slowly. Food was not plentiful. The barracks, stretching as far as you could see through the huge POW camp, were cold and drafty. Blankets were hard to come by. Many young men, suffering from deep depression, elected to charge the electric fences to take instant death by electrocution, rather than to endure the harshness of their fate.

"There's a young man you should see," whispered one POW to Clair. "He's an American, in a barracks not far from here. He's talking about suicide."

It was again Christmas Eve—this time, 1944.

Clair found the nineteen-year-old downcast and huddled on his bunk.

"What's the use," said the dejected young man. "We're gonna die here anyway—why not get it over with."

Clair sat beside him.

"No, you don't want to do that," said Clair, "This is Christmas Eve. This is the night that hope was born, not a time for hope to be lost."

The young man was quiet.

"Do you like music?" asked Clair, trying to get his thoughts onto something else.

"Yeah, I used to play the saxophone," he murmured.

"Really. I love the sound of a saxophone," said Clair, beginning to move the young man's attention away from his woes, and into a conversation between two American servicemen away from home.

"You married?" asked the young man.

"Yes, I am," said Clair, "Would you like to see her picture?"

He nodded, watching Clair pull a picture of his wife from his wallet. Something else in Clair's wallet fell to the floor. The young man leaned down and picked it up. It was another picture.

The young man was astonished.

"Where did you get this?"

Nobody was more surprised than Clair. For a long, speechless moment he absorbed the miracle that had just unfolded before him, and took a mental snapshot of the face of a young man who—minutes before—was contemplating suicide; a young man now exuding joy as he gazed at the picture of the young waitress from California—his fiancée.

Hope was truly born on Christmas Eve.

The rest of the story? Both Clair and the young man returned home safely to America. The young man and the young waitress were married. And, according to letters received by Clair, they lived happily ever after.

Karen & Franco—
Love in the Middle of the Ocean

Karen Gold lived the dazzling storybook life that young girls omnivorously read about in *Cosmopolitan*. She was the beautiful Wilhelmina model smiling her way through flashy New York parties attended by the likes of Andy Warhol, dodging Broadway paparazzi on the arm of football great Joe Namath, and courted by a string of famous or not-so-famous-but-rich-and-handsome guys.

What could be greater?

She was not only *living* the life others dreamed about, but she had the best of both worlds: a powerfully successful career and the joys of motherhood—two babies from a prior marriage.

What could be greater?

Freedom.

That's what she determined she needed. To be free. Free

from shallow smiles and people who wore them. Free from everyone who wanted something from her. Free from the world of glamour and its cutthroat underbelly.

She needed a break.

Quickly accepting her mother's offer to take the children, Karen agreed that she needed to get away. To find some place where there was no one she knew. No one to place demands on her.

At La Guardia Airport she dragged her bag from airline to airline, studying the menus of exotic destinations.

Puerto Rico? No.

Acapulco? No.

Maui? No.

Freeport?

"Freeport? That's it! I want to be free!" she said aloud.

Franco Ferrandi lived the storybook life that boys dream about: a successful maître d' at the Princess Hotel in the Bahama Islands. For seven years, since leaving his native home of Milan, Italy, Franco opened his eyes every day to a landscape of clear blue water and long sandy beaches. He had a job where beautiful young women approached *him*, asking *him* questions.

"What do I wear for dinner?"

"A beach towel. [Pause. Smile.] My dear, you would look wonderful if you were wearing only a beach towel."

"Would you have a table for two at eight?"

"Yes, my dear. [Smile.] I can be available at that time."

It was never a case of *would* he have a date that night—it was *which girl* would he date.

But something was beginning to happen. The fast-track life was beginning to wear thin.

It was his day off. Franco jumped on his dune buggy and headed for a white stretch of deserted beach. "I wanted to be by myself," he said.

Karen had no idea where Freeport was. Never heard of it before. She just got on the plane.

Upon landing, she asked a cabdriver to take her to a nice place, somewhere near a faraway beach. And, almost as soon as she checked into the charming little inn, Karen headed for the beach with nothing more than a copy of *Rolling Stone* magazine.

Ahhhh.

Peace and quiet.

Nothing like toasting your back under a hot sun as your toes wiggle into the sand and the only sounds are distant seagulls muffled by a lazy, tumbling surf. Yes . . . *this* was the feeling of *free*.

Vrrrooom. Vrrrooomm.

An unpleasant noise pierced the peace, closer and closer. Then, quiet.

Lifting one squinted eye, Karen could see bare feet. They were standing a few feet from her. She considered the options: should she turn over and see who it was, or just play possum?

"I don't think you are British," said the friendly male voice with a pleasant accent. "No, if you are reading the *Rolling Stone*, you must be American."

So began a conversation that segued into a ride on the dune buggy to a "better" beach, and a weeklong companionship with a man who Karen found to be handsome and kind.

"He had a nice way about him," she said. "I found myself laughing a lot."

Karen liked Franco and she was mildly surprised with his nonchalant response to her up-front disclosure that she had two small children back home.

"I love children," quipped Franco.

This acceptance of something that would strike terror into the hearts of most single men seemed all the more sincere when, after her return home, Franco sent Karen two small bracelets, a popular item in the Bahamas that Karen had admired on other children, but was unable to find in any shop.

The courtship evolved.

Over the course of several trips back to Grand Bahamas Island, Karen and Franco began to fall for each other. Still, saying "I love you" was a big step for Franco.

"Love is a big word," says Franco, "I never wanted to use

that word unless I knew I really meant it. Yet there were so many things I liked about Karen. Her good sense of humor. I liked the way she enjoyed taking care of me—those take-charge qualities that came from her being a wonderful mother. Then, one day, I just said it, 'I love you.' "

Three decades later, Franco still says, "I love you," every day.

Two people madly in love, now with three grown children, still living a storied life with summers on Martha's Vineyard and winters in Palm Beach. But occasionally they let their minds drift back to earlier years. Unquestionably, their lives today are eminently more satisfying than when they were beautiful people on the fast track exalted by movies and magazines.

They marvel at how each arrived at a feeling of running-on-empty at the same time, how each was drawn to a desolate stretch of sand in the middle of the Atlantic, and how they found each other because of the word "free" in Freeport.

Divine intervention is divine

The best thing about being the author of this book is to see how joyful blessings have unfolded in the lives of people, and knowing they can be repeated in your life. How, as Jhannea and Chad's preacher noted, their power bill must have been misdirected by a divine power to bring them together; how a picture in Clair Miller's wallet, placed there in California, brought hope to a despondent young soldier behind enemy lines; and how Franco and Karen's paths were divinely orchestrated to intersect on a lonely beach in the middle of the ocean.

There's a quote I have always enjoyed from Sir Hugh Walpole: "The most wonderful of all things in life, I believe, is the discovery of another human being with whom one's relationship has a glowing depth, beauty, and joy as the years increase. This inner progressiveness of love between two human beings is a most marvelous thing. It cannot be found by looking for it or by passionately wishing for it. It is a sort of divine accident."

The Difference between Hope and Expectation

If you start every day with the expectation that it is going to be a great day—it's different than *hoping* it will be. That's the mind-set I would like you to adapt. Go into every day with the total expectation that the desires of your heart are *going* to be fulfilled, that you are *going* to achieve the goals that you've set for yourself, and that you are *going* to find the love that you deserve.

Adapt this as your habit, and you can expect many unexpected godwinks!

7

Mapping Your Godwinks

"How do I read the signs—the godwinks—leading me to my soul mate?"

"Are they telling me—this is the *one?*"

"Should I be making an on-the-spot decision, radically altering the rest of my life?"

These are the kinds of questions most of us ask when a godwink occurs in the midst of developing relationships. Sometimes, rather than clarifying matters, we wonder if an incredible coincidence is "telling us" something, urging us, by unseen forces, toward a particular action.

As I have said, godwinks are not directives.

They are signposts of reassurance, guiding you in making your *own* free will decisions. You must continue to listen to the small, still voice within—your intuition—and make the important choices in your life on your own, bolstered by an awareness that you are surrounded by the invisible safety net of the Almighty, confirmed by godwinks, that you are never alone.

When you reach threshold moments in your life, those times when you experience an event, encounter someone, or make a life-changing decision that sets you off onto an entirely new path, there are always godwinks. They are there like signs at the fork in a road. You may notice them and shrug them off. Or you may be so involved in the new experience that you fail to notice them altogether. But they are there.

If you can take the time to do a sort of archaeological expedition into your past, first recalling the threshold moments, then thinking about godwinks that you overlooked or forgot about, you can begin to map them.

While a single coincidence is a signpost, a *continuous pattern* of godwinks—multiple coincidences flowing in a distinct direction—is a *map*.

It's hard to see the trees when you are standing in the middle of the forest. But when you observe your life through the wider perspective of hindsight, consistent patterns of godwinks will emerge with greater clarity; you will begin to understand that a map of godwinks has all the while been directing you along your path to your rightful destiny.

In two stories that follow, I want to take you through the circuitous lives of two couples who, today, look back upon the continuous flow of godwinks they experienced as confirmation that they were meant to be.

At the end of the chapter you'll see how each couple's map distinctly materialized, helping you better to understand how to map the godwinks in your own life.

Jane and Rick's long road to love

She was twelve. He was thirteen.

Were they destined as soul mates? At that moment, they had no way of knowing.

Jane Ubell was a guest at a Bar Mitzvah in Great Neck, New York, held simultaneously at one venue by the families of two young men. Jane's friend was reaching a significant threshold in a Jewish boy's life. A coming of age. The boy in the other family celebrating this significant moment was Rick Meyer.

Were Jane and Rick supposed to meet that day? We don't know, but it's the first time that they were both in the same place at the same time.

Three years after that Jane was casually introduced to Rick in the schoolyard by a friend who whispered that Rick was a tennis star, one of the best on the East Coast. As she shook his hand, Jane, a five feet two bundle of joy, smiled and made a mental note: "Too tall. Not interested."

A decade later, in 1980, both Jane and Rick's lives had followed paths of successful career development. She was a bright, twenty-three-year-old segment producer at *Good Morning*

America and Rick was a twenty-four-year-old tennis pro—
ranked 80th in the world.

Jane was at Flushing Meadows for the annual U.S. Open
Tennis Tournament. Settling into her seat, she did not realize
she was about to see her former schoolmate, Rick Meyer, play
John McEnroe on center court. It would have been nice to say
"hello," but there was no opportunity. Only by hindsight did
she realize that happenstance had placed her at a second
threshold-moment in Rick Meyer's life—the first being his
Bar Mitzvah; this time, the day he took on the world's number
one tennis player, John McEnroe.

Two months went by. Jane was having dinner in New
York's posh Upper East Side eatery, Jim McMullen's. Just back
from a seven-week tennis tour, Rick Meyer also just happened
to be there. The type of guy to never forget a face, he spotted
Jane and approached her table.

"Jane Ubell! I'm Ricky Meyer . . . we went to high school
together!"

Slightly reeling from his enthusiasm, and feeling somewhat awkward about this conversation in front of the date she
was with, Jane cordially handed Rick a business card.

"Hey . . . she's really cute," said Rick to his friend, back at
his own table.

The next day he followed up with a phone call. They
arranged their first date at the Metropolitan Museum of Art.

Several dates followed. "Sometimes we went out . . .

sometimes I cooked dinner, and we spent the evening at my apartment," said Jane. "Ricky would bring over a great bottle of wine and we'd listen to Barbra Streisand's newest album."

Their favorite song was "Evergreen."

After a few months, Jane knew she was falling for him. In fact, she was crazy about him. Inside she heard what she described as an authoritative masculine voice: "Hey . . . stop looking. This is the one!"

But as much as Rick liked Jane, he knew he had another commitment—his tennis career was the primary focus of his life. And he was about to be on tour for months. In reality, he couldn't allow himself to become involved in a relationship.

They parted.

Jane was crushed. But she moved on.

Four years passed.

Jane, at twenty-eight, accepted a job in Los Angeles on the syndicated program *Entertainment Tonight*. She loved L.A. Everything about it. She had no desire to go back East. She threw herself into her job.

Rick stayed the course on his tennis career until age thirty-one. He met a girl; they married and had a child.

Eight years later, in the spring of 1988, Jane returned from the West Coast to visit her father and stepmother. En route to a matinee Jane sat in the backseat of a car once again enjoying the sights of New York.

Out of the blue, Jane's stepmother, Marsha, asked, "Whatever happened to that tennis player?"

"Well . . ." hesitated Jane, turning to look out the window. Her heart stopped!

"There he is!"

Rick was sitting in a car right next to theirs, stopped at a traffic light. They simultaneously spotted each other and rolled down their windows.

"I can't believe it!" shouted Rick. "They're playing our song."

Astonishingly, at that very moment, Rick Meyer was sitting in a car listening to the radio. Barbra Streisand was singing the song "Evergreen," which had taken his mind back to the happy times, years earlier, when he and Jane had heard that song played repeatedly while dating.

"How *are* you?" she shouted, her heart leaping.

"I'm married and I have a baby boy," he blurted.

Jane's heart sank—somewhere below sea level—notwithstanding the oh-I'm-so-happy-for-you look on her face.

Traffic moved on. Rapidly the remarkable godwink vanished like Rick's car in the rearview mirror. Absently gazing into the hubbub of the city, Jane reflected, "Rats. He married someone else. . . ."

Eight years passed.

Jane tried to say that she was "over" Rick, but she never

seriously got involved with anyone else. This, despite the focus of everyone else in her family who seemed to be more obsessed about her romantic status than she was. As far as she was concerned, work was a fine substitute for relationships.

Jane's career moved from TV show production to producing films. Her biography of Leona Helmsley, *The Queen of Mean,* won wide audiences and Emmy nominations, and her independent films were well received at the film festivals. But, upon completion of her third film, a production that was particularly arduous, she told her partner, "I've had it with filmmaking."

After the wrap party, she continued with friends to a local bar. Within moments of her arrival, an outgoing young man wearing a surgeon's scrub shirt came through the front door and headed directly to her. It was as if he were on a mission.

"Hi . . . I'm a pediatric surgeon," he playfully said to Jane.

She laughed, thinking, "Now there's a great opening line."

He then admitted that he was a screenwriter.

"Where are you from?" he asked.

"New York."

"Where in New York?"

"Great Neck."

"Great Neck!" he repeated, "I have a cousin who grew up there. Ricky Meyer."

"Ricky Meyer! . . . He was the *one!* I always loved him," she exclaimed, suddenly cautious that her feelings were showing.

"Forget about him. He's happily married and living in Westchester, New York."

Again, Jane's heart sank. Yet . . . here was another god-wink associated with Rick Meyer. What are the odds that a stranger would come up to her and turn out to be Rick's cousin? And this time, the godwink was at a threshold in *her* life. Only a half hour earlier she had decided to completely change direction and quit film production. Here she was, standing on the precipice of uncertainty about the next steps in her career. All she knew was that she loved living in L.A.

A few weeks later the cousin called Rick. "Hey, I saw an old friend of yours . . . Jane Ubell. I told her you were happily married."

"Not true! I'm going through a brutal divorce!" said Rick. It was the month of March, 1996.

"I was home alone. The phone rang," said Jane. "My heart stopped when I heard his voice: "This is Ricky Meyer.""

After several minutes of catching up, Rick asked, "Do you ever get back East?"

"You won't believe this," she said. "I haven't been back for Passover for twelve years. But, this year I am! I'll be there next *weekend*."

"Really. Well . . . how do you like living in California?"

Before she could answer, she again heard the internal voice, the same masculine voice that, years earlier, had said, "He's the one." This time the voice was insistent.

"Tell him that you're thinking of moving back to New York."

"What??" she argued inside her head, "Anyone who knows me knows I would never move away from L.A.!"

"Tell him!" said the voice.

"Yeah . . . I like California . . . but . . . I'm thinking about moving back to New York."

Inside, she snapped at the voice within, "How can I lie like this?"

They arranged a date for the following Friday night in New York.

"I was so nervous about seeing him again," said Jane. So many years had passed since their last coincidental meeting—two cars stopped at a traffic light on 57th Street—just as he was listening to "their" song.

"I was so nervous I developed a twitch my right eye," she said, adding, "Is that a godwink or *what?*"

As the date approached, the twitch got worse. Her friends and family reassured her that no one could tell, but she didn't believe them.

Friday night, 8 P.M., and the doorbell rang.

Jane's eye began twitching frantically.

"Ricky walked in. He was so handsome. Hair slicked back.

Leather jacket. Tight jeans. I felt like a teenager," she said, trying to disguise her twitching eye.

The date was flawless. They couldn't stop talking, catching up and laughing. And all evening long Jane's eye wouldn't stop "winking" at Rick. Eventually she acknowledged it. He confessed he'd noticed it. And they had a huge laugh about it.

Jane remained in New York for a week. They saw each other several times, but—as she was quick to emphasize— "only as friends." Jane could feel a reawakening of deep compelling feelings toward Rick, but she was cautious. She had never forgotten the pain of earlier disappointments.

"He has baggage," she argued with herself. "He's still wending his way through the divorce. He has two kids. Besides— I love California."

Jane's father was bent on rebuilding old bridges. "If you won't tell him to come over for Passover dinner, then I will," he insisted.

Across the table Jane's aunt Evie exclaimed, "You two look like you have been together your entire lives!"

Leaning to Rick, Jane whispered, "You were very brave to come here tonight."

A few days later Jane returned to the West Coast. They stayed in touch, and in less than twelve months, she finally gave in to the inner voice: "This is the guy."

She moved back to New York.

*　　　*　　　*

Fast forward to April 2000.

Jane and Rick had been inseparable for four years. Jane had grown to love New York again, and started a new marketing business.

Rick had become a successful executive in the world of finance and his divorce was three years behind him. But he had concluded that it was time to be decisive. So, he laid a trap. Selecting a week when Jane said she needed to be in Portland, Oregon, on business, he told her that he also needed to be out of town that same week, on business, to Paris.

"Paris?" said Jane, "You can't go without me! I'll cancel my Portland trip!"

What she didn't know was that the trap was already set and tickets were bought. He had counted on her canceling her trip.

In Paris, Rick took Jane to the Eiffel Tower. After their tour of the tower, he "spontaneously" suggested they go to a café nearby. And in that romantic atmosphere, Rick unveiled the question, "Since we are such great partners, how would you like to be a senior partner in the firm of Meyer and Meyer?"

Jane started to cry and said, "Yes."

Reaching into his pocket, he produced the ring.

Again, she cried.

On September 16, 2001—five days after the tragedy of

nine-eleven—and at the insistence of their rabbi, who advised that their faith commanded that life must go on, they were married in Westchester County, New York.

Their wedding turned out to be more intimate than planned, because the closed airports throughout the world kept so many friends and relatives away. Jane's mother, for instance, who lives in San Francisco, was able to participate in the ceremony only by cell phone. But, for Jane and Rick, it was the most special day of their lives.

Their marriage was the appropriate outcome to thirty-two years of signposts—the unfolding of a marvelous map of multiple godwinks, continuously suggesting that they were "meant to be."

They are deliriously in love.

Your road may not be as long

Let's hope that the road to your love won't be as long as Jane and Rick's. That was a long path to finding each other. But, because of other choices we make in life—often like trying to jam together two puzzle pieces that don't fit—we get off the path that was intended for us.

Has that happened to you?

Please take a few moments to study the following chart. See how Jane's and Rick's paths can be laid out on a map. They intersect at various points, until eventually, godwinks brought them together.

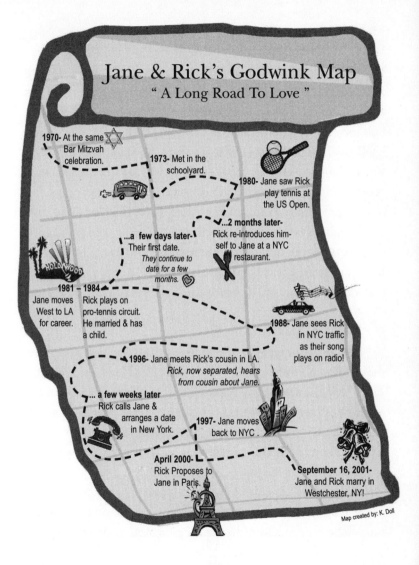

Jane & Rick's Godwink Map
" A Long Road To Love "

1970- At the same Bar Mitzvah celebration.

1973- Met in the schoolyard.

1980- Jane saw Rick play tennis at the US Open.

...2 months later- Rick re-introduces himself to Jane at a NYC restaurant.

...a few days later- Their first date. *They continue to date for a few months.* 💗

1981- Jane moves West to LA for career.

1984- Rick plays on pro-tennis circuit. He married & has a child.

1988- Jane sees Rick in NYC traffic as their song plays on radio!

1996- Jane meets Rick's cousin in LA. *Rick, now separated, hears from cousin about Jane.*

... a few weeks later Rick calls Jane & arranges a date in New York.

1997- Jane moves back to NYC .

April 2000- Rick Proposes to Jane in Paris.

September 16, 2001- Jane and Rick marry in Westchester, NY!

Map created by: K. Doll

Parallel Tracks to a Match Made in Heaven

I've already talked about how my wonderful wife, Louise DuArt, and I fell madly in love and married, nearly thirty years after I happened to be in a position to recommend her for her first job in television. But what is really interesting is looking back over that thirty-year map—now so much clearer with hindsight—to see the parallel signposts and godwinks that seemed to have been nudging us toward each other, preparing us for a predestined union somewhere down the road.

Imagine two little kids, born miles apart.

Louise entered life on October 30, growing up in Quincy, Massachusetts. I was born on October 31, a few years earlier, and raised in the small, northern New York town of Adams Center.

Two little kids with dreams.

Louise dreamed of being in show business. She tells how she was deeply influenced by her favorite television program, *The Carol Burnett Show*, costarring Tim Conway and Harvey Korman. When her mother would give her a quarter, sending her to the Catholic church to "Light a candle for lost souls," Louise would light the candle and instead pray, "Please God . . . please just let me meet Carol Burnett."

A little girl's dream. A little girl's prayer.

Whatever guilt she may have felt about not praying exactly as was expected of her was eradicated years later when, one day, the phone rang and it was Carol Burnett herself! An incredible godwink! Carol had come across a videotape of Louise doing an impression of her, and couldn't resist calling to invite Louise to lunch.

Just picture Louise getting that phone call from her heroine, and the thrill in realizing that her little girl's prayer *was actually answered!*

Today Louise jokes that as she exited the Disney Studios commissary where she had lunch with Carol Burnett, she lifted her eyes skyward and said, "Thank you, Lord, Thank you. Now . . . if I could just . . . meet . . . Tim and Harvey. . . ."

Proof that someone really *is* up there listening, came ten years later, in much the same manner: the telephone rang and this time it was Tim Conway!

Another godwink had placed Louise's videotape into *his* path at the very moment he was looking for a comedienne who could go on tour with him and Harvey Korman in a show called *Together Again*, featuring great sketches from *The Carol Burnett Show*.

Louise's emphatic acceptance barely allowed Tim to complete the question.

For several subsequent years, the little girl from Quincy who fantasized about being on *The Carol Burnett Show*, Louise DuArt has starred with Conway and Korman in as many as one hundred performances in a year.

When you consider the events that happened to Louise, it

is difficult not to shout, "Wow . . . what are the odds of that!" But even more so when we look at those godwinks on parallel tracks with the extraordinary events that had happened in *my* life.

In book one, *When God Winks*, I told my story—the young boy, raised in a farm community near the Canadian border of New York State, whose dreams of broadcasting were ignited by a visit to a radio station during sixth grade. Subsequently, during almost every waking moment, I practiced speaking into a broom handle mimicking my hero, an announcer on a radio station miles away, Dean Harris, who urged his morning listeners to "get up and march around the breakfast table."

From that dream emerged a remarkable godwink.

On the day I was en route to my first job interview in broadcasting, at age fifteen, I was picked up hitchhiking on a lonely country road by none other than my *hero*, Dean Harris!

For years the power of this coincidence continued to resonate in my mind—*what are the odds of my getting picked up hitchhiking, on a rural road, by my hero?*—until I came to understand that it was really a powerful signpost along my path, a message of reassurance from above that I was doing just fine, to keep the faith, that everything was going to turn out all right.

My *getting* the job that day really underscored the significance of godwinks as signals of reassurance in our lives, because that initial job was the beginning of a fabulous career in broadcasting that took me all the way to the top levels of ABC.

As discussed earlier, I was the vice president of Children's and Family Television at ABC when Louise DuArt first came into my consciousness. She was featured in a live stage show at Madison Square Garden in New York, produced by Sid and Marty Krofft. I took my daughters Robin and Hilary to see the show.

Totally by coincidence, three or four weeks later, I was meeting with the Krofft brothers to develop programs for the ABC Saturday morning schedule. As we began to think about comediennes who might be cast for a rock group we were putting together to wrap around all of our shows, I suggested that we take a look at the girl who played Witchiepoo that I'd seen in the Kroffts' own *H.R. Puf-n-stuf* show.

The parallel events—Louise being in that show; my taking my daughters to *see* that show; and, totally unrelated to that, my being in dialogue with the Kroffts about developing television programs—led to my eventually meeting Louise three decades before we were able to become reacquainted and marry.

In comparing notes more recently, we have come to realize that there were many godwinks that prepared us for our destinies, our eventual matrimony and missions together.

In our early twenties each of us had read and were greatly influenced by the inspirational teachings of Dr. Norman Vincent Peale in his book *The Power Of Positive Thinking*. And just how coincidental do you suppose it was—that a few months before I began writing this—we were both invited to join the board of Guideposts Publications, founded by Dr. Norman Vincent Peale?

When reflecting upon the parallel tracks leading us toward an ultimate intersection, Louise and I began to appreciate that we had met and befriended some of the same people along the way; people who unbeknownst to either of us were influences upon both of our lives.

In my first book, I described in detail how Louise was discovered at a comedy club by *Star Search* scouts who *just happened* to be there at the same time, to audition someone else. They cast her in the nationally televised program, and just as Louise was doing her *Star Search* performance, singer Donna Summer *just happened* to tune in. This initiated a remarkable chain of godwinks resulting in Louise becoming Donna's opening act, and traveling with her on the road for the next two years.

Meanwhile, I met Donna Summer through entirely different circumstances, through Seal Kasha, wife of composer Al Kasha, eventually becoming friends with Donna and her family, visiting their New York apartment and Westport, Connecticut homes. Yet, Louise and I never knew that we both knew Donna Summer, until years later.

We also learned that we had both hired the same producer. As Louise's career grew, the Showtime Television Network offered her the opportunity to produce and star in two television specials. As she was lining up staffing for the second of these productions, her public relations adviser, Marleah Leslie, recommended a former colleague, a producer she had worked with on *Entertainment Tonight*, Gary Grossman. Louise loved working with Gary and said he was one of the best producers she'd ever known.

Quite by different circumstances, I had also found Gary Grossman to be a wonderful producer. At the time, I was in charge of ABC Late Night Programming seeking to develop a suitable show to follow *Nightline*. I came up with an idea for a show called *Day's End*—a live, daily one-hour program that played clips and segments from shows on various television networks; sort of a digest for busy people who were unable to see TV that day.

I knew I needed a producer who was quite extraordinary. Doing a live show made up of clips from other shows from that very day meant you could pretty much forget about advance planning.

My friend Vin DiBona, producer of *America's Funniest Home Videos*, recommended Gary Grossman. It took some selling to convince Gary to leave Los Angeles and move to New York City, but it turned out to be highly auspicious for both of us.

Gary Grossman and his lovely wife Helene became my friends.

All the while, I had no idea that they were also dear friends of Louise DuArt.

Louise and I had also—quite independently—befriended Tony Orlando. I got to know Tony when I invited him to host a late-night talk show pilot. That friendship was enhanced by Tony's involvement in a musical video I created for ABC Children's Television called *The Kingdom Chums*, in which he sang and provided the voice for the lead character. (Believe it or not, the giveaway of that video subsequently played a role in Louise landing a daily TV talk show on ABC Family Channel.)

Louise, it turns out, was introduced to Tony through Donna Summer. Several years after their initial meeting, Louise and Tony were performing in Atlantic City at the same time, and a mutual friend invited them both to dinner. Tony mentioned that his former variety series for CBS had just been picked up for rebroadcast by a cable TV network that was being run by an old friend of his—SQuire Rushnell. Louise lit up. "I know SQuire . . . he gave me my first job in television," she exclaimed.

By coincidence, less than eight weeks later I happened to show up backstage at a Broadway show in which Louise was starring. It was a day when I was supposed to be out of the country. The trip was canceled. But that was a good thing, because Louise's show was also just canceled; I was attending the final performance.

We went for coffee that day, and have rarely had a day since when we *haven't* had coffee together.

After we were married, the parallel threads that seemed to weave Louise and me together became more and more evident. As we put our household furnishings together, we became conscious that we had exactly the same taste in furniture—English antique—and we have both collected old clocks all of our lives.

In unpacking boxes, I noticed a familiar videotape label used by a one-person production studio in New York. "You've used Peter Klusman?" I asked.

"Yes, my former manager found him," she replied.

"I've used Peter for years," I said.

Shaking my head, I marveled at the extraordinary way our paths were intertwined; it was genuinely spiritual.

We had just unpacked photos of our dads and talked about how much we wished they could have gotten to know each other. They both had died *on the same day*, three years apart. My dad died on *November 13*, 1988. Louise's father on *November 13*, 1991.

Both of our dads loved carpentry, and they both enjoyed ending their workday with a bottle of beer. By now our dad's have surely met—they're up there watching us—each holding their favorite, a Pabst Blue Ribbon beer.

*   *   *

In *When God Winks* I wrote that one of the most significant coincidence stories I ever heard was the one which ignited my interest in studying coincidences. It was that the two presidents who had more to do with the Declaration of Independence than any other—Thomas Jefferson and John Adams—both died on the same day. It was not just any day—they died on the fourth of July, 1826—the exact fiftieth anniversary of the most important event in each of their lives: the signing of the Declaration of Independence.

I wrote that Jefferson died in Monticello, Virginia. Adams died at his home in Quincy, Massachusetts.

I remind you that Louise was born in Quincy, and grew up just blocks from John Adams's home.

Now think about this: my series of books were birthed by events relating to John Adams, and I was born in Adams Center, emphasis on Adams.

Your own Global Positioning System

It is not at all surprising when you look back on your life, with the clarity of hindsight, to see clear patterns—how signposts of godwinks were erected at certain points, as you moved from one place to another in a marvelous mosaic of free will and God's will.

If you list all of those significant crossroads and signposts, you will be astonished at what has happened to you when you weren't looking. And you will come to better understand the perspective I have spoken about, that you are on a sort of Global Positioning System—a GPS—that has helped to navigate you through life.

Mapping Godwinks to See the big picture

We so often wonder: "How do I really know there's somebody up there watching over me? Besides, with six billion people on this planet, how can I be sure that my voice is getting through?"

Mapping your godwinks and seeing how your life has followed a more orderly path than you may have imagined, will reassure that your voice *does* get through.

Mindful of the people and events in the story you've just read about Louise and myself, please take a careful look at the map that follows. I am hopeful that our experiences will validate that you also have trackable occurrences that fit neatly into God's bigger picture of your life.

Louise & SQuire's Godwink Map

"Parallel Tracks To A Match Made In Heaven"

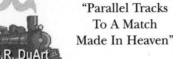

R.R. DuArt

R.R. Rushnell

Born OCTOBER 30th Quincy, MA.

Born OCTOBER 31st Adams Center, NY.

At age 11, she imitates people and
dreams of meeting Carol Burnett.

At age 11, he dreams of
radio & TV.

Godwinks

New York City- First Sighting at Madison Square Garden
Louise performs on stage as Witchiepoo.
SQuire sees the show.

She's cast in Krofft's
ABC Saturday AM show.

He recommends her for Krofft's
ABC Saturday AM show.

Star Search leads to her
tour with Donna Summer.

He develops ABC show
with Tony Orlando.

Louise meets Tony Orlando and
then her hero Carol Burnett.

SQuire and Donna Summer
become friends.

She stars in *Catskills On Broadway*.

He attends *Catskills on Broadway*.

New York City- Another Sighting
SQuire encounters Louise backstage at *Good Morning America*.

Godwinks

She stars in *Dreamstuff*
on Broadway.

Merge

Scheduled to be out of the country,
he sees Louise's in her closing
performance of *Dreamstuff*.

New York City- Love Is Brewing
After *Dreamstuff* SQuire invites Louise for coffee.

**Louise and SQuire date 4 years
and are married on October 28, 2000**

Map created by: K. Doll

8

Meant to Be

This is such an important point, it bears repeating.

If the whole universe consists of concepts of the Creator that are predestined to fold together in perfect harmony—from the changing of the seasons to the fluttering wings of a butterfly—why wouldn't God have intended an ideal mate for you?

As I mentioned before, the Yiddish language has a word that means "intended one." It is *bashert*. In a deeper interpretation, it means that your intended one was predestined before birth.

When using that language, one would say: "That is bashert!" when you wish to denote that a particular relationship or event is intended by destiny.

Or, you might say, "I am searching for my bashert"—

suggesting that you are looking for the person for whom you are intended.

In the true-life stories that follow, Debrah and Greg, Jennette and Meyer, Carol and Harry, and Herman and Roma, all had to search for their bashert. I think you will see that they were surely "meant to be."

Debrah and Greg: The actress and the director

"I don't think I was born to be an actor," says Debrah Farentino, now putting other things higher on her priority list—things like motherhood, being a good wife, and reading fat college textbooks on molecular biology.

Others felt differently. Agents, managers, publicists—the kind of people who flocked to a beautiful, ebullient actress who made a splash in her role on the CBS soap opera *Capital*. They perceived a traditional arc for the birth of a star: glamorous roles, popping flashbulbs, and big hair.

"They sent me only one script that I *really* liked," she confessed, "It was this girl who played opposite John Ritter in a Steven Bochco series for ABC, *Hooperman*. She was the kind of character who loved books, wore overalls, and had short hair. My kind of girl—no pantyhose, no hot curlers, no big hair."

Debrah was reading the script en route to a film shoot in Italy. Then, upon landing, she was told that the part was already cast.

"But I liked that role. So I . . . someone who never saves

anything . . . saved that script, and when I got back to L.A., I heard the producers had decided to recast for the role."

Her agent confided, "This part is not for you. They're not interested in a soap actress."

"Hey, let me read anyway!" she insisted.

A reading was set.

She was to read a scene with John Ritter for Steven Bochco and his Producer/Director Gregory Hoblit.

Debrah decided she needed to "get into" the role. The day before the reading she did what she thought the character would do: she went to a bookstore. Scanning a wall of books, Debrah spotted exactly the book she thought her character would have reached for.

She reached up for it.

At that moment *another* hand reached up for the very same book.

Pulling it off the shelf, she turned to look at the other person.

It was John Ritter.

In a flash, she knew something *he didn't* know: that the next day she would be sitting across from him in an audition. A thought struck her—to make the moment secretly memorable to Ritter.

"Just *why* would we *both* be interested in this book?" she laughed, holding it up. She departed.

*   *   *

Greg Hoblit was Steven Bochco's secret weapon. For every hit series that Bochco sold to the networks—from *Hill Street Blues* to *LA Law*, from *Hooperman* to *NYPD Blue*—and many in between, Hoblit was the director, the producer, or both.

Hoblit didn't like the idea of having to recast for *Hooperman*, but he and Bochco felt they had to. Once again they had to commit many hours to the difficult process of reading actresses for the part.

The day was nearly over.

Then, "Into the room came a rocket ship!" said Hoblit, "A dynamic whirlwind—Debrah Farentino." He smiled, recalling his first impression of the girl whose beauty, sense of self, and personality would touch his soul for years to come.

Debrah hated auditions. She felt she didn't do well at them. But this time, carrying the prop for the part—the book she had purchased the day before—she confidently advanced to the front of the room, greeted John Ritter, and began the reading.

They were into the reading when Debrah, premeditatedly, lifted the book to emphasize a point.

In a blink, Ritter connected. He recognized the book *and* the girl holding it. His mind flashed to the coincidence of the day before—he and this girl both reaching for the same book, at the same moment. It was something very special. A godwink.

"The book helped me to connect with John in a way that dissipated my fear," says Debrah. "And it must have worked. They cast me for the role."

Only by hindsight can we now understand that Debrah was at a crossroads in her life. Not only was she getting the part in *Hooperman*, she was getting a long-term part in the heart of Gregory Hoblit.

Over the course of the series a comforting friendship would grow deeper between Debrah and Greg.

"The thing I always felt about him on the set was his very kindhearted manner," says Debrah. "I like him."

Greg's perspective: he was genuinely intrigued by Debrah. He never felt crowded by her. As someone who was guarded, one of Hollywood's longest-running available bachelors, a guy with a reputation for immersing himself deeply into every film and program he supervised, Greg liked the way Debrah gave him his space.

There was one brief period when they got to see each other with greater regularity. Greg was shooting in New York, and Debrah had returned there to resume studies in premed. While their affection for each other may have been deepening, they both knew the timing wasn't quite right. Then, before they knew it, they were back on the fast track pursuing their lives and careers.

Over the next several months Debrah met someone else. She married him, and soon she was an expectant mother.

Still, Greg Hoblit was the friend she liked to talk to.

"When I had my first baby, he was the first person I called up. I said, 'This is great. Hoblit, you ought to do this.'"

Of course, she didn't mean *they* should have a baby together, but she wished her *friend* could also experience the joy of having a baby.

Over subsequent years Debrah's marriage ended, and she and Greg attempted to stay in touch. Yet, as they tried to get together from time to time for coffee, their plans seemed to always fizzle when one or the other had something come up at the last minute.

"It was a given. Our paths always seemed to be diverging rather than converging," said Greg ruefully. "Then, after this one get-together for coffee was canceled, I decided to give up. Right after that, I got a surprise."

The more introverted of the two, Greg would always gravitate to places of low visibility. He'd heard about an exercise gym in a West L.A. office building basement—a room not larger than a one-car garage—where a trainer had established a workout center suitable to Greg's liking.

Debrah had also heard about a small gym that had a wall where she could practice her rock climbing.

Same place.

She showed up for her first appointment.

Greg was just leaving.

That coincidental meeting—which wouldn't have happened if Greg had departed thirty seconds earlier—provided the second pivotal godwink between them.

"What about that cup of coffee?" Greg asked.

"How about right after my workout?" replied Debrah.

The coffee date turned into dinner. And out tumbled saved-up conversation.

"I've been thinking that my friend Diane would be perfect for you," said Debrah. "You should meet her. She's wonderful. My best friend from before high school."

Greg looked at her.

"I'm interested in *you*," he stressed.

Oh. That changed things.

They began dating.

"It felt comfortable," said Greg. "I was forty-seven years old and I had never found anyone who made me feel safe. She had become a parent and I liked her maturity. She was grounded."

"Molly and I are a package deal," said Debrah over dinner one night. She spoke with a frankness so as not to be misunderstood, just in case Greg was thinking of anything more serious.

He *was* thinking seriously. With every woman Greg dated,

he had always asked himself, "Would I like to be a family man with this person?" The answer was never "yes," but, with Debrah, the answer was an easy "yes."

"That peace of hers . . . that certitude . . . there it was . . . just clear!"

It was in a romantic setting in Sun Valley, Idaho, where the pensive, well-prepared movie director, against a backdrop of years of thought, made his spur-of-the-moment judgment. He asked Debrah to marry him.

"No," she said.

"Why?"

"I'm not ready."

"Okay."

But a short while later she said, "Yes. I like the idea."

Looking back upon fifteen years of friendship—nine as a married couple—Debrah and Gregory now see with clarity that the paths they traversed were not nearly as ambling and ad-lib as they once thought. They see the symmetry. Their meeting and marrying were meant to be.

The godwink at the crossroads of their initial meeting—Debrah and John Ritter reaching for the same book in a bookstore—and then the godwink that placed Debrah and Greg at a small gym in an office building basement at the same time, can now be viewed as signposts directing their paths.

When I spoke with Debrah and Greg individually, I asked

them to each name the three most important things in a successful relationship. Neither hesitated a moment to answer.

Debrah said:

1. Kindness. You must constantly display kindness to your partner.
2. Integrity. It's the trust that allows you to "just know" that he is there for you.
3. Passion. Not just romantically, but having passion in everything you do: being a mother, your work, or allowing your partner to have passions of his own.

Greg said:

1. Listening. Really hearing each other.
2. Integrity. A clear, unwavering moral center.
3. Acceptance. Accepting each other for who they are, not who you *want* them to be.

About listening and understanding

Greg's comment about listening—really hearing each other—gives me an opportunity to point out something my wife and I discuss in a seminar we do called "LOVE LAUGHS: Everything I Know about Wrecking Relationships I Learned in My Last Marriage!"

Have you ever heard yourself say, "You don't *listen* to me?"

I think what you really mean is, "You may be listening with your ears, but you aren't really *understanding* what I am trying to communicate to you."

In successful relationships, men and women find a way to show that they are clearly paying attention to each other; sometimes by repeating what their partner has just said, in different words, to exemplify that they were both listening and understanding.

This is an even more important practice for men. While women, by nature, need to talk things through—to process them—we guys have this caveman tendency to want to go right out and conquer the problem, to get to the bottom line. We have to hold ourselves in check. To listen. To understand. As Greg Hoblit says, to show that we are "really hearing."

A word about how we reveal answers

Greg Hoblit was unusual. He was an unbridled bachelor for almost fifty years. Yet, like most people, the answers to what it took for Debrah to tame him were revealed in his own words.

Repeatedly he said, "She made me feel safe." Not in a secure sense, but "safe" in that she was never crowding him. She gave him plenty of space.

Greg is just like every man I know. Even if he's aware that a woman desires to lead him down the bridle path to matrimony, he never wants to feel that he is losing his "space."

Debrah, intentionally or not, never gave Greg indications that she was trying to catch him. In fact, she even told him he ought to meet her friend Diane. And she was not always available for coffee dates.

My mind goes back to my earlier discussion about the film *The Horse Whisperer*. When Robert Redford wanted to catch the wild stallion, he didn't chase after him. That would have been the worst thing he could have done. He gave off an air of determination and confidence, but also placed himself in a lower position and quietly waited for the horse to come to him.

Men are attracted to women who are independent. Who can stand on their own. Who are not needy. Greg saw Debrah as a self-reliant mother. He admired the way she balanced her work, her continued studies, and motherhood, yet was able to give him undivided attention when she was with him.

In a way, she got her man through good horse sense.

Back to bashert

True life stories give us hope that even if we haven't yet found the perfect fit for the piece of the jigsaw puzzle called "My Life," it will happen.

In the following story, Jennette and Meyer had to endure more than ever should be expected of two human beings living in a civilized society. Yet, as I suspect you will agree, they were intended for each other.

Jennette & Meyer: A Story of Faith

"Oh, Meyer, I do love you," whispered eighteen-year-old Jennette on her wedding day.

Her love for Meyer was growing everyday. He was older, stronger, and made her feel safe. He was a kind man who loved talking about having children and a family. And, she admired how he had helped so many others, smuggling them across borders, escaping death.

Jennette and Meyer said their marriage vows in Budapest, Hungary, a safe haven—they thought—from the atrocities that were happening to other Jewish citizens in their native Poland and other countries occupied by the Nazis.

It was 1943.

While still in Poland, Jennette was narrowly sent, on several occasions, to Auschwitz, a notorious concentration camp where over two million people perished. But each time, the buses filled up, and by coincidental timing, she was left behind.

Jennette then fled to Hungary where she met and fell in love with Meyer Ehrlich.

Only weeks after their marriage, Jennette was able to tell her husband the joyful news that she had felt the stirrings of a baby inside her body. Anxious to father a child, Meyer was thrilled.

But Hungary was not safe.

The Germans ominously moved into the country and assumed control without firing a single shot. Again, Jewish people were being rounded up and taken away.

Several months into her pregnancy, Jennette and Meyer were dining one night in a restaurant. Hungarian police marched in and ordered identification from various customers. Jennette's heart stopped as they demanded to look at Meyer's papers.

"He may be an underground terrorist," said one officer.

"Take them in," commanded another.

At the police station, it was determined that Meyer would be sent to Munich to be put on "trial"—which everyone knew was only for show—and that his fate almost certainly meant that he would be sent to another horrid concentration camp, Dachau, where most prisoners were put to death.

Noticing that Jennette was pregnant, the police ordered her to remain behind for "questioning." Jennette was terrified. Yet, from the moment she saw her husband being jostled away by authorities, she never doubted that he would survive.

She prayed. And she had faith.

Meyer had told her about his earlier survival, before they had met, from his incarceration in Auschwitz, and subsequently at another labor camp; how he and a group of others had been shot in their escape, and how he was able to get away despite a bullet wound to the neck.

He *would* survive, she believed.

* * *

Jennette saw an opportunity to sneak away from the jail.

She ran.

In Budapest she was able to make contact with someone who said they could help her get to Romania. Now, at nearly full-term pregnancy, she was smuggled across the border with a small group of others. In Romania they felt great relief when they saw a Jewish name on a house.

They knocked.

"Quickly—come in," said the owner, looking in both directions.

Leading them inside, he said, "Make yourself comfortable. Take a bath and have something to eat. I must go out. I will be back with more food."

Within the hour police burst through the door and arrested them. To protect himself, the owner had betrayed them.

Jennette was taken to a camp.

Again, she saw a way to escape.

Again she ran.

She encountered a lady taxi driver who offered to take her to the docks.

"Someone will help you," she was assured. "They will take you secretly aboard a livestock ship to Constanta."

The ship would take her to the Romanian seaport through mine fields in the Black Sea.

As the ship sliced through dark waters, Jennette could see

the shattered remains and debris from an earlier ship that had detonated a mine, spilling its passengers into the cold depths of the Black Sea.

She began to feel labor pains.

Ill-equipped to assist in the birth of a baby, the captain sent out a coded signal. Another boat came alongside, and took Jennette ashore in Turkey. There, because she was Jewish, she was made to sign papers that when the baby was born it would not be identified as a Turkish citizen. At a nursing home, she gave birth to a boy. His name was Charles.

Told she could remain in Turkey for only one month without a visa, Jennette made her way back to Israel. She took training, and became a nurse.

A few months later her hopes soared when a small box came in the mail. But when she opened it, her dreams plummeted. Inside were Meyer's personal effects . . . and ashes.

"He is dead," said a friend of Jennette's. "No one escapes Dachau."

"No. He is a survivor," said Jennette, with conviction, while choking back tears, "I do not believe those are his ashes. I believe he is still alive."

Nearly two years passed.

Another man who had once been with Jennette in one of the small groups smuggled to safety had also found his way to Israel. His name was Bernard Teichtal. Long attracted to her, Bernard now professed that he had fallen in love with her.

"Will you marry me, Jennette?" asked Bernard.

She declined.

Later, Bernard repeated his request.

Jennette's friends were insistent.

"Jennette, your intuition is wrong. Meyer is gone. You are being foolish. Bernard is a good man. He loves you. Marry him."

Reluctantly, she said she'd consider it.

Jennette suggested that Bernard find an apartment, and used other excuses to delay a decision. Deep in her heart she believed—she *hoped*—that it was her *friends* who were wrong, not her. For, every time she looked into the eyes of her twenty-two-month-old baby, she could see the face of her husband.

When her friends became relentless, Jennette finally accepted Bernard's proposal and set a date for the wedding.

Four weeks before the ceremony, Jennette was waiting at the bus stop on her way to work. She noticed a Red Cross flyer that was posted there. Written in Hebrew, it said the Allies had freed the prisoners of Dachau and listed notices of people who had been separated from their loved ones.

Jennette's mouth dropped as she read: "Meyer Ehrlich, Munich, looking for his wife."

She fainted.

People at the bus stop rushed to her aide: "Poor thing. She hasn't had breakfast—look how thin she is," they said.

Jennette came to.

She looked at the poster again.

She fainted again.

It was almost beyond belief—her faith that her husband Meyer was still alive was rewarded!

"I am so happy!" she said.

Jennette quickly contacted her fiancé Bernard and told him that she was sorry, but the wedding had to be called off. She told her friends that she had to find a way to get to Munich.

She packed her bags, bundled up baby Charles, and made her way to Paris. There she was told that there was one train that could take her to Munich. She bought tickets.

But the train failed to stop in Munich. There was no way to get off. Like it or not, Jennette was bound for Vienna.

Options raced through her mind. She had endured so much. To be so close to her beloved husband, and not to succeed in reaching him, simply wasn't an option.

She was determined.

When the train slowed to a stop ten miles outside of Munich to take on water, Jennette seized her opportunity. Tightly holding her baby, she slipped unnoticed from the train, leaving all her belongings behind.

For several hours she dodged oncoming trains, and stumbled on rocks and railroad ties.

"Momma," said little Charlie, "I would like to have a piece of bread."

"Just a little further, my baby, and you will have all the bread you want."

Darkness was falling as Jennette and little Charlie made it into Munich. Someone directed her to the home of Meyer's brother, only to receive another disappointment: Meyer—in his search for her—had gone to Paris.

His brother immediately sent Meyer a telegram.

In a matter of days, her prayers came to pass. Jennette, her baby, and Meyer were back in each other's arms. And that is where they remained for many happy years to come.

Jennette and Meyer moved to America, had two more children—a brother and a sister for Charles.

Still speaking with a slight accent, Jennette says, "I love this country. Every day I say a prayer to God. To say thank you."

In 1990, twenty years after relocating to America, Meyer died.

Seven years later Jennette saw Bernard Teichtal, the man she left at the altar. It was a brief conversation. He was dying of cancer.

"I always loved you," Bernard told her. "I never married. And, because I was with you during your pregnancy, I always thought of Charlie as my own child."

It was a bittersweet closing to another chapter in Jennette's life. But, more heartfelt than most, she can attest to the power of godwinks that arise from a deep and determined faith.

Jennette never doubted that she and Meyer were bashert—intended for each other.

Carol Channing is just wild about Harry

"I was so in love with Harry I couldn't stop hugging him," says Carol Channing, describing her affection for the thirteen-year-old boy whom she loved when she was twelve. "It was thrilling and sweet to have his arms around me."

Writing about her childhood sweetheart in her autobiography, the famed actress and Broadway star characterized Harry Kullijian, the son of an Armenian immigrant, as "disciplined."

"In hindsight," she says, "I realize how disciplined he was and what a sense of responsibility he had."

Harry established a strict moral code for the two of them, allowing almost no time together during the week, away from their studies, and maximizing their time together on weekends.

"It was the most difficult thing in the world not to make love to Harry," Carol confesses. "I just wanted to be close to him and hug him." Recalling Harry's disciplined manner, she smiles coyly, adding, "But he would distract me."

Once Harry confided to Carol's parents how affectionate she was with him, quickly offering assurances, "I will never get your Carol into any kind of trouble."

"I like that boy," said Carol's father, "I like that boy."

Carol Channing and Harry Kullijian went steady all through junior high school.

Having the outgoing personality of a future star, Carol was the one who had initiated their meeting when she asked Harry to dance. When she learned that Harry was the leader of the school band, she asked him to help her create a song for her campaign to be student vice president.

Harry took charge. They created a compelling, memorable jingle that had the whole school humming, "We want Carol, we want Carol . . . When I'm vice president, we'll all leave school at twelve o'clock."

She won.

But when Carol and Harry became enrolled in two different high schools, some distance apart, they had less time to spend with each other, and their relationship became more distant. Still, Carol would miss Harry—his comforting, confident manner.

"I remember the day I lost a debate," recalls Carol in her wistful trademark voice. "I thought, 'Oh, if only Harry were here, he'd know what to do.' Then, my wish came true! Harry pulled up in his car and said, 'Hop in, let's take a drive.' He was such a dear. Just a sentence or two from Harry would set me right."

Carol went on to become an actress in New York. Awed with the bigness and brawniness of Broadway, there were times when the rejection of a failed audition caused her to wish Harry could once again manifest himself. "Arriving in his car, out of the blue, Harry would know just what to do."

Carol's and Harry's lives moved on from the embers of first love. They each developed new friends, new relationships, and new geographic identities. Each became only a memory to each other. Harry met another girl, Gerry; they fell in love, and had a wonderful sixty-year marriage until she died in 2002. Carol was twice divorced and once widowed, yet emerged from each marriage with a sense of lovelessness.

On several occasions over the years Harry tried to contact Carol, proud of her accomplishments, starring in such Broadway shows as *Hello, Dolly* and *Gentlemen Prefer Blondes*. But he always had difficulty getting past the gatekeepers. Once, as a serviceman on leave in New York City, Harry went to the theater of a sold-out show and stood before the poster of his childhood sweetheart. He saw a limo pull into the alley and caught a glimpse of Carol entering the stage door, while the man who was with her stayed behind. Harry quickly walked up to him. He said he was an old friend, that they had gone to school together and had even gone steady. But the man— Carol's husband—said no, he couldn't see her.

By the time Carol's book, *Just Lucky I Guess*, was published in late 2002, Harry was a distantly fond remembrance. She wrote about their teenage romance, wishing she'd gotten to see him again somewhere along the line, during the intervening seventy-year period. She assumed he had died—she was 82, and he would have been 83. And men have shorter life spans than women, she reasoned.

Though Carol had many times witnessed that faith could lead to the fulfillment of the desires of her heart, she couldn't imagine that it could happen to her again, at this stage in her life. What she didn't know was that there was an unwitting messenger—a Godwink Link—who was about to lead her life onto a whole new path.

Mervyn Morris, owner of Mervyn's Department Stores, was that link. He had long been a Carol Channing fan. In college, he and two pals were discussing what they wanted out of life; one speculated that he wanted "to be a lawyer in England," the other, "to be a big producer." Mervyn spoke as though he had long rehearsed it: "I want to run my father's stores and marry Carol Channing." That comment started a fabled adoration of Carol that extended over decades, as members of his family showered him with Carol Channing photos and memorabilia. "Don't you have space on your office wall for one more Carol Channing photo?" they would tease.

For his eightieth birthday Mervyn's family contacted Carol, asking if she could make a special guest appearance at his party and dispatched a private jet to pick her up. It was a tearful event. Mervyn was thrilled, and grateful, to meet his heroine.

It was therefore no surprise that Mervyn Morris was one of the first people to go out and buy Carol Channing's autobiography in the fall of 2002. As he read about Carol's teenage love for Harry Kullijian, he jumped. He knew Harry—they had done business deals together!

He immediately got busy tracking down Harry.

"Harry, did you know that Carol Channing wrote about you in her book?" Then he counseled, "Harry, you should call Carol. Her birthday is on January thirty-first; she'd love to hear from you. Here's her number."

Mervyn then picked up the phone and called Carol.

"Harry and I are friends," he told Carol, who was astonished Harry was alive. "Please look for his call."

Mervyn Morris was the Godwink Link. He also represented the best description of a modern-day Cupid.

Harry wasted no time. "When I called," says Harry, "I found I was only a couple hours away from her place near Palm Springs, California." When she said, "When are we going to get together?" Harry said, "How about tomorrow!"

Their meeting was joyful, cautious, curious, electric, bashful—any number of adjectives.

For two weeks after that first meeting they spoke several times by telephone, two or three hours at a time. Then they had a date. And before long they were talking about marriage. A date was set, and three and a half months after they had reconnected, they were married on the day before Mother's Day, 2003. Where did they take their vows? No place other than the home of their Godwink Link, Mervyn Morris, would do. He had insisted.

On occasion Harry has reflected on one other godwink. It happened just before he received that life-changing call from Mervyn telling him that Carol had written about him in her book. Elise Schneider, a college president who had been an old friend of Harry and Gerry's, had also said, just days before, "Why don't you call Carol Channing?"

Harkening back to the discipline he displayed during their teenage years, Harry has brought his business acumen and organizational skills into Carol's life, assisting with her schedule and activities. But—mindful that he once told her parents "I will never get your Carol into any kind of trouble"—he is most proud of his spiritual initiatives in their marriage, leading daily prayer and looking heavenward for guidance. Harry notes that they have a pure basis for their union—that Carol was faithful in each of her marriages and he in his.

For both Carol Channing and Harry Kullijian, the wonderful godwinks that happened to them—and the Godwink Link of Mervyn Morris bringing them together after reading Carol's book—were the bellows that rekindled seventy years of dormant love.

With great confidence Harry says, "God brought us together."

Herman and the apple girl

"How long can I go on in this cold—without food—without hope?"

Herman, a thin, teenage boy, shivering as he shuffled behind the barbed wire fence, was motivated by the thought that any movement of his frail body could keep him from freezing to death.

He had been dumped into a concentration camp along with millions of other poor souls, just because he came from a Jewish family.

It was winter, 1942.

"I'm so hungry," he whispered, conceding that his words would only evaporate hopelessly into the cold morning air, just as his breath was doing. Everything around him was so stark it was like being in a black-and-white movie. At a happier time in his life that would have been a funny thought, walking around like Charlie Chaplin. But not here. He was now in a place where humor was given a death sentence just as surely as the one that he and his fellow prisoners were facing.

He expelled a sigh, condemning another whiff of breath to disappear into thin air.

There was no hope.

Perhaps it was the slight movement that caught his eye. He turned. Staring back at him through the barbed wire fence was a young girl. She was expressionless. He wondered how long she'd been looking at him.

He stepped closer to the fence. She was younger than he.

Perhaps she came from a middle-class family. But there was something about her . . . a mysteriousness.

Then she moved slightly, slowly placing her hand into her pocket. It emerged, holding a red apple.

In one rapid swoop, the girl threw the apple into the air . . . up . . . up . . . over the wave of wire at the top of the fence, landing with a thud near Herman's feet. Promptly he picked it up, cradling it like a treasure in his cold, cupped hands.

For a moment he gaped at the prize, then lifted his eyes to his benefactor, astonished.

She smiled. And ran away.

An apple was such a small meal, but in Herman's predicament, it was a holiday feast. Slowly he nibbled at the apple, savoring every juicy bite, even crunching the seeds and the core.

Was she heaven-sent, wondered Herman? Was she real? She must have been, for his satisfied stomach was proof.

The next day Herman awoke, questioning if he could even dare to hope that the girl would reappear. He returned to the same spot near the fence. He waited. Hoping that if she did come back, that he wouldn't be seen by the Nazi guards. And he surely wouldn't want her to get into any trouble, either.

She was pretty. As far as he could tell from his memory of her staring at him, she looked kind—yes, her smile, just before she ran away—that meant she was kind.

Glancing to see that no one was watching him, he edged near to the barbed wire fence. There was no one. He was about to feel dejection. But then, there was movement. His eyes widened as he peered through the barbed wire and saw the young girl step from the shadows, moving like an angel floating from a cloud.

Again she dipped into her coat, produced an apple, and with the deftness of the day before, swung her arm upward, tossing the apple up, up and over the wire, descending this time, with a smack, directly into Herman's frail palms.

Herman had asked for nourishment and hope. God replied through the young girl who continued to visit him, nearly every day, for seven months.

Then, one day, he was told that the Germans were shipping him and others to a different camp. Were they lying and really sending him to the ovens or gas chambers? Was this his death sentence?

That day as he waited for the young girl at the fence, his heart was heavy. He would miss her terribly.

"Do not bring me an apple tomorrow," he said, when she arrived. "I am being sent to another camp. We won't see each other again."

Certain that he was about to cry, he ran from the fence. He didn't look back.

But during the many months that followed, his indelible memory of her sweet smile and the kindness of her heart sustained him as he endured yet another concentration camp.

*   *   *

When they heard armored vehicles approaching, one day, sounding different than the German army trucks, Herman's hopes began to rise. It was the Allied forces. Herman was freed from captivity.

Everything was lost—his family, all possessions—everything. But he had the good memory of the apple girl, and now, his freedom.

In a few months Herman was able to join others who were boarding a ship bound for America. There he could start a new life. And that's what he did. He was able to find work in New York City. And though he never found anyone he wished to marry, he was able to make a comfortable living. He had friends. And a nice couple would occasionally invite him to their home for dinner.

One night, his friends had invited someone else. A woman named Roma. She was a pleasant conversationalist, and seemed quite interested in what Herman had to say.

"Where were you during the war?" she asked gingerly.

"In several concentration camps," he replied, naming them.

A faraway look seemed to develop on Roma's countenance. She spoke, as if she were picturing something in her mind: "I once lived near a concentration camp. There was a boy there—I visited him every day—I would bring him an apple."

Herman could not believe what he was hearing. Was it possible that he, again, was about to witness a miracle?

"Did . . . the boy ever say to you . . . 'don't bring me an apple tomorrow'?"

"Yes," said Roma, brightening.

The two adults looked into each other's eyes, seeking an image of the young person they once saw.

Roma smiled. That special, sweet smile.

And Herman *knew* it was her.

His voice quivered as he cupped his hands around hers, just as he once held the treasured apple that she'd given him.

"Roma, I have thought of you daily, and held you in my heart for years. This moment is more than I could have ever dreamed. I cannot let you go again. I want to be together with you forever. Will you be my wife?"

Again she smiled that sweet smile.

"Yes . . . yes I will, Herman."

They held each other tightly for a long time, choking back joyful tears, as a godlike spirit seemed to move between them.

How can we ever doubt that we are on a giant Global Positioning System in the heavens that can save us from hopelessness and nurture us with happiness?

Do you know people who are bashert?

Look around you. There may be couples you know whose stories could have just as easily been told in this chapter. You may now see them in a different light. Perhaps you always felt that they "made a good couple," but never saw them as two people whose lives were perfectly intersected by celestial controls.

They most likely were meant to be. Intended for each other—bashert.

To have and to hold

The stories in this chapter bring to mind a question that I long wondered about. I pondered the meaning of the marriage vow "to have and to hold." What does it really mean? Does the word "hold" mean to physically hold, as in hug? Or to hold hands?

I have come to conclude that while a tactile connection is important with your partner, the word *hold* really means to "hold up"—to honor. To place your partner in a higher position than you place yourself. To put them first.

Ask any partner in this book, "Who is the most important person in this couple?" and I imagine they will say, unequivocally:

"He is."

"No, she is."

9

Godwinks Through Inanimate Objects

It's natural to think of *people* as the Godwink Links who come in and out of our lives, unwitting messengers of joy, that I spoke about earlier. But sometimes the Almighty uses inanimate objects as the catalytic force to bring people into line with the paths that have been predestined for them, causing an alteration to their course.

When a godwink happens through a *thing*—a coat, a book, a snapshot, a locket, or a song, as it does in the stories that follow—and that object becomes the link to something or someone who changes our lives, it can seem odd, serendipitous, or almost humorous by hindsight.

If you're the person in the middle of one of those uncertain states, not sure whether you are in love, or wrestling with decisions that need to be made, it may seem as though God is having a good time at your expense.

In the end, the people involved in the following stories each viewed the uniqueness of the godwinks with a positive, good-natured outlook.

Bruce and Renee's black coat of many colors

It hit him like a ton of bricks. He had absolutely no idea *this* was going happen to him! And *here*, of all places? She took *this* time and opportunity to turn his life upside down?

To anyone on the outside, Bruce Jacobson had been leading a charmed life. A lovely wife, two kids, and a glamorous TV job subsequent to his stint at the Reagan White House; he was an active leader in his church and his wife was an equally involved member of the choir.

It was a picture-perfect model family.

Sure, he knew his marriage could use a tune-up, but nothing that couldn't be fixed with a little counseling. In fact, that's why he kept insisting they meet with a matrimonial counselor—to lay matters before a trusted third party and get their marriage back on track.

But, *here?* She took this moment—a meeting with the pastor—to serve him with divorce papers?

*　　*　　*

For months Bruce grieved. He grieved for the loss of someone he loved—not in death—but it seemed the same. All the same symptoms: shock, anger, uncertainty.

"How can this be?" he kept asking himself. "This is wrong."

The teachings of his faith led him to believe that divorce was unacceptable. He had meant those words: "Until death do us part." But now it was as if he had sinned in the eyes of his church, and he had no control over it.

Worse, people at church now seemed to avoid him. It was like he had something contagious. Where were the calls of support from his pastor . . . or anyone else in church? Didn't they understand? *He* didn't cause this to happen. *He* tried to fix it.

There was some good news, however. Bruce would never be totally adrift in a time of crisis. He had his mom and dad, and six brothers and sisters; they were a tight family. They regularly talked, they could pray and support each other, and they had wonderful traditions they always kept—like Christmas shopping, for instance. For as long as he could remember, Bruce and his family would set aside one special day to do their Christmas shopping together.

Bruce's sisters Jan and Julie worried about their brother. They prayed for him. They asked members of their Bible study group to pray for him. Julie's best friend Renee offered to pray for him. Renee was like another member of the family. In fact, Bruce always thought of her as another sister.

Renee earnestly prayed that Bruce's wife would reverse her decision—that their marriage could be healed.

What was the moment, Bruce wondered? The exact moment that he ceased seeing Renee as a sister, and began looking at her differently—as a wonderfully kind and attractive woman, never married, and with the same values and beliefs he held?

As time went on, Bruce and Renee saw more and more of each other. He really liked her. No, he really was falling in *love* with her. But—why was he holding back? What was he afraid of?

Months went by, and they saw each other still more and more; they were clearly an item to others.

Two years went by. Renee was patient. Bruce was clearly fearful of making any commitment to anyone—the pain of rejection, betrayal, and unfairness was still too close to the surface.

It was just before Thanksgiving.

Bruce and Renee were strolling through Nordstrom's in an upscale shopping area, not looking for anything in particular. Renee stopped. A coat on a mannequin just stood out and seemed to beckon her. It was beautiful. She tried it on. The coat's long black leather lines and its fox fur collar looked tailor-made on her. The fit was perfect, a medium, she noted. As she twirled before the mirror, the alternatives danced in her mind: yes, she needed a coat; no, she was not actually looking for one right now; no, how could she ever afford *this* one; she'd never spent $1,200 on a coat.

She took it off.

"Would you like us to hold it?" inquired the saleslady. "A deposit will hold it . . . and this is a very popular item this year," she continued.

Renee was torn.

"Wellll . . . how long can you hold it without a deposit?" she asked.

"Only twenty-four hours. But if you like, I'll put your name on it and put it in the back till tomorrow."

"Okay," said Renee. But as she and Bruce left the store, she dismissed the coat as anything she could afford.

Five weeks later Bruce returned to the shopping mall, this time as part of his annual tradition of Christmas shopping with his mom, brothers, and sisters. What should he get Renee? he wondered. Then it came to him . . . how about the coat? Yes. That would be perfect . . . more than he planned to spend . . . but wow, wouldn't that be perfect. He returned to Nordstrom's. The sales clerk who had waited on Bruce and Renee the month before was nowhere in sight.

"I'm looking for a black leather coat with a fox fur collar, in a medium," he said to another saleslady.

She laughed . . . a knowing laugh . . . like it was a private joke.

"Those are all gone," she said. "Those coats were this year's most popular item."

"Are you sure?" asked Bruce, disappointed. "Another salesperson held one for us."

"Did you leave a deposit?"

"No . . ."

"Let me tell you how sure I am," she said confidently. "A lady was in here and said she'd pay three hundred dollars over the price tag just to get one in a medium. I called every store in the state and couldn't find one."

"All right," said Bruce, dejectedly departing.

Outside the store he stopped. "Wait," he said to his mother and sisters. "I just have to ask one more time."

Returning to the saleslady, Bruce said, "I know you'll think I'm crazy . . . but could you just humor me? Could you please just take a look in the back?"

The lady sighed, resisting the urge to roll her eyes. She paused.

"Please? I know it's silly . . . but if you could just humor me, please?"

With a slight shaking of her head, she disappeared into the back.

The next image will always be imprinted in Bruce's memory bank. The playback is in slow-motion: the lady returns, her arms raised high like an Olympic athlete who has just completed the event in record time, a triumphant smile upon her face, and held high in her outstretched arms . . . is a black leather coat with a fox fur collar!

"I . . . I . . . can't believe it," she stuttered. "How could this be? These coats were all gone."

Attached to the cuff was a small handwritten note: "Renee."

It occurred to Bruce sometime later that in the Bible of his faith, a coat had frequently been used as an important symbol: "If your enemy asks for your hat, give him your coat," counsels one passage. Then there's the story of Joseph's coat of many colors, the one that metaphorically evolved into a Broadway show.

In a way, Renee's black leather coat represented the many colors in Bruce's life. The colors of a happy new chapter.

The almost miraculous appearance of that coat in the saleslady's arms was a monumental godwink . . . a powerful message of reassurance for him to have faith, to move on with his life, and—without fear—to ask Renee what he really wanted to ask her:

"Will you marry me?"

And just to be certain that his proposal would have a lasting impact, Bruce secretly arranged with Dr. James Robison and his wife Betty, hosts of the show that Bruce produced, to pop the question to Renee, in the studio, on camera, in front of a live audience, and a televised audience of millions around the globe.

Renee glowed with surprise and joy when she realized the dimensions of what was happening. She had no hesitancy in her reply.

"Yes . . . yes I will marry you."

Ron and Marion—Godwinks and patience

Ron Russell never forgot his childhood sweetheart.

"Marion was my girl," that's all there was to it. Except . . . it took nearly eighty years, and some wonderful godwinks in a Burnley, Lancashire secondhand bookshop, in England, for them to get together.

He now wonders, "What if I had not convinced my son Graham to take me on a nostalgic visit to my childhood town of Burnley?" It had been fifty years since he'd been there. As they browsed in the small bookstore, Graham came across a book titled *Looking Back on a Lifetime in Old Burnley*, by Marion Rudd.

"Do you know this woman?" he asked his father.

Shocked to hear the name of the only girlfriend he had never forgotten, Ron stood, stunned, looking at her name on the book. In his mind he could clearly visualize the beautiful young teenager he had once loved so much. And remembered how heartsick he felt when his family moved to another city.

"Yes," he lamented quietly. "But I imagine she's dead by now. After all, I'm eighty-five, and she was a year older."

"No she isn't!" remarked the store clerk who overheard the conversation. "She lives nearby, and I have her telephone number."

Ron's demeanor brightened.

Calling up right away, he invited Marion to dinner. It was a wonderful reunion. So much in common. So many memories to share.

"We have my daughter to thank," said Marian, long divorced from her first husband. "Linda convinced me to write the book, and to use my maiden name. Just think . . . if I had used my married name we'd never be here right now."

Comforted by the godwinks that had brought them together, a brief courtship was all that was needed before taking their vows in a charming wedding at Upton Village Church, near Gainsborough.

Asked if he had any difficulty in recognizing his sweetheart after nearly eighty years, Ron promptly replied, "Not at all. When I saw her, I knew her . . . by her twinkling eyes."

Ron and Marion's story reemphasizes that in the jigsaw puzzle of life, finding the perfect fit—the perfect mate, written into our destiny—sometimes requires considerable patience. But, harkening to the godwinks that are sometimes delivered to us in most unusual ways—such as an inanimate book in a shop—assures that we are on the right path.

In another place in Great Britain, there was a comparable story.

John and Shirley: sandcastle memories

Shirley remembers the long sandy beach in Somerset, England, and the sounds of the gulls and the surf on hot, sunny days when her mom and dad would take her there. She loved to dig in the sand, and build castles suitable for the queen. Then, years later she could relive those moments through snapshots taken by her father.

Shirley grew up and moved miles away, eventually settling in Horsham, in Sussex. There she met a wonderful man, John Peskett—they fell in love, and married. John was everything Shirley had ever dreamed about: he was handsome, kind, a good provider, and a wonderful father.

Was he the perfect prince, intended by destiny to share the castle of her dreams? She thought so—not certain—but, thought so. A sign of confirmation would have been nice.

One day Shirley sat with John, showing him photos from her childhood. They smiled at images of the small girl building a large sand castle on the beach.

John suddenly had an astonished look on his face.

"That's me!" he exclaimed, pointing to a boy on the beach in the photo, just past Shirley.

"How do you know?" she said, lighting up.

"That was my fav'rite swimsuit, and that's my mum sittin' there on the blanket."

They were able to confirm that, yes, both had spent summer days of childhood on the sandy beach of Somerset.

"Oh, John," said Shirley, hugging him, "I knew it. I knew we were meant for each other."

A small snapshot had provided the godwink of confirmation.

Elaine Garrett's secrets of the locket

"Where's Charles?"

That was the question not only on Elaine Garrett's mind as the young bride-to-be continued to glance at the clock on the church wall. It was also what was causing the guests in the front of the church to wiggle in their seats and whisper, "What could have happened?"

The worst thing that could happen to a bride on her wedding day was to be left standing at the altar by her groom. That's what Charles did to Elaine.

Eventually his absence sank in—for his parents, who had flown out to Denver from Illinois just for the wedding; for the others who began to trickle out of the church; and finally for Elaine, the broken-hearted bride . . . still waiting.

Over and over, she questioned, "What did I do wrong? What happened?" as she sequestered herself at the local YWCA.

The next day, Elaine received a phone call. A drunken man started to speak, then a woman grabbed the phone to announce, "I'm going to steal him from you."

"You can have him," said Elaine, slamming down the phone with finality.

She never heard from Charles again.

She did wonder from time to time if he had shipped off to war in the early 1940s. If he had been killed. And she wondered what he did with the small heart-shaped locket she'd given him with their two pictures in it.

Mostly, she tried to forget the pain.

But she never could.

The pain of rejection at the altar was like a recurring toothache, way beneath the surface, lingering for decades— through her successful marriage to James Gamble, which lasted more than thirty-four years until his death.

The pain continued to lurk like a bad dream in the back of her mind until September 2002, when she had a visit from her granddaughter, Susan Gamble, from Pennsylvania. That was the day that Susan brought her a gift—a small heart-shaped locket.

When Elaine opened it, she was astonished. There was

her picture at age eighteen. And there was the picture of the lout—Charles.

"Where did you get this?" she asked her granddaughter with a tone of disbelief.

Susan explained that she had been searching the internet for World War II memorabilia as a gift for a friend. She spotted a locket from an estate sale in Georgia—a gold locket for three dollars. That was too good a deal to pass up. She bought it.

When the locket arrived in the mail, Susan showed it to her dad, James Gamble. He looked at the original photos inside, and asked, "When did Grandma give you this?"

"She didn't. I just bought it on the internet."

They could hardly wait to show it to Grandma during their visit to Oklahoma the following month. Yet, they could never know that the locket—a nearly worthless inanimate object—was really a priceless key for her.

When Elaine Gamble held the locket in her hands, all the old emotions poured from their hiding places: the embarrassment of being jilted at the altar, the anger with Charles for letting her down so badly, the years of uncertainty as to what had gone wrong.

The return of the locket was a blessing. For years Elaine had harbored the notion that she had done something wrong. That she was the cause of the shame that had been brought upon herself and her family. But the unbelievable odds of the locket coming back into her possession was a godwink of release and closure for her.

"It was a sign that everything is going to be all right—not to carry those old thoughts anymore," she says quietly.

Godwinks help you to leave your baggage behind

Sometimes it is so difficult to let go of the guilt that we carry around like shabby old worthless baggage, loaded with ancient pain and resentment. We keep it as a possession because we think we're supposed to, or because we think we can't get along without it, or because we're just used to having it weigh us down.

If you're in a relationship that is loveless, stuck, and going nowhere, think about mentally throwing your baggage into the trash and moving on with your life.

Get up tomorrow morning and say these words: "Nowhere does it say that I do not have the right to happiness!"

Go claim it.

Mari and Bill: words and music

"When I fall in love . . . it will be forever . . ." sang Nat King Cole on the radio as little Mari Falcone practiced her piano lessons in Chicago.

It became her favorite song as she trained as a classical pianist and achieved her master's degree in music at the University of Miami.

Mari's musical career blossomed—conducting for Donna Summer, playing for Amy Grant, and serving as musical director for such star performers as Debby Boone, Nell Carter, and others. But as she talked with her girlfriends about her ideal husband, she preferred that he wouldn't be a musician at all, she hoped that he'd have "at least a master's degree," and that the song playing at her wedding would be *that* one: "When I fall in love, it will be forever."

She also had a clear picture of the guy she had in mind.

"Certainly no one like that geeky-looking guy in the band, Bill Cantos!"

Was he looking at her?

The sweetness of Bill Cantos's personality was a fitting companion to his honey-laced singing voice.

As the band's keyboardist, he *had* been secretly attracted to Mari Falcone. His surreptitious glances were perhaps telltale signs of an infatuation that was growing within. He admired her strong Italian trait to say what was on her mind and to take charge. Long after their musical sessions, his memory would focus on her image—her beautiful mahogany-red hair, framing an angelic face.

At first, their telephone conversations were all business.

But Bill sensed he was beginning to cross a line into a more personal way of speech.

Mari built defenses against any equal attraction. Her head struggled to maintain complete control over her heart. And Bill Cantos, she feared, was liking her just a little too much.

One weekend the Los Angeles area endured a small earthquake. So did Mari.

She called a few people, including Bill, to see if they were all right. He was fine, he said, and on his way out of town. He'd call on his return in two days. But, for the next two days she became bewildered and agitated with her own feelings.

"I miss him and I don't even *like* him," she argued with herself.

Upon his return, Bill invited her out for a bite to eat. They chatted easily about their pasts and their dreams for the future. Bill loved singing, composing, and arranging, he said, and had been trained at the New England Conservatory where he earned his master's degree in music.

"Oh no!" was Mari's internal response. "A master's degree is one of my prerequisites for a guy. Not *this* guy!"

Catching Mari slightly off guard, Bill asked, "Do you have a sense of where this relationship is going?"

Instantly, Mari's voice inside said, "I just like you as a

friend, Bill." Yet, her *external* voice used different words: "Let's just take it slow."

"What? Take *what* slow?" responded her internal voice, sounding shocked.

"You don't even *like* this guy!"

A week or two later, Bill invited Mari out again on the eve of his leaving town for another assignment with one of the top jazz bands. As the evening ended, her external voice was again saying something her internal voice would never have approved of—something silly.

"Sing me a song good-bye, Bill."

He sang her his favorite song. The one with more meaning than anyone could possibly know. The one he had always told people that when he met his perfect love, she would love it, too.

He sang, "When I fall in love, it will be forever. . . ."

"I *knew* you were going to sing that song!" exclaimed Mari, tears glistening in her eyes, and marveling at the wonderful godwink that was occurring.

Mari began rethinking her earlier misconceptions about Bill as the "geeky" guy in the band. She suddenly could not understand why it had not been clear to her before—he really was a very *attractive* man. For now, it was *unmistakably clear* that this was a man who was not only beautiful on the *inside*, but handsome on the *outside*, as well.

Over the course of several dates Bill continued to wrestle with his feelings. He and Mari were different than each other's expectations for a perfect mate.

"Isn't there supposed to be a clap of thunder—a sign of some sort—something out of the blue that says, 'Hey kid, this is the *one?*' " he questioned.

He was sitting on his bed, absently clicking through TV channels with the keypad. As he tuned through the Country Music Channel he stopped. His eyes widened. As if answering the question he had just been asking, K.T. Oslin was singing a song about two people who really loved each other, despite their different expectations for a mate: ". . . that's why Willie doesn't have a woman . . . and that's why Mary doesn't have a man . . . ," she sang.

That was it! His godwink of reassurance!

Here at the exact moment he was wondering if "Bill and Mari" were the perfect match, he randomly tuned the TV to a song about "Willie and Mary," a couple who were grappling with the same issues.

Things were suddenly clear. In two instances, a powerful force from above had used music—a language unique to both Bill and Mari—to send a message of reassurance: the coincidence of "When I Fall in Love" being the favorite song of both, and now, a K.T. Oslin song featuring two people similarly named "Willie and Mary."

Bill began planning how he would propose. He put a lot of thought into it.

"How can my proposal be memorable?" he pondered.

"Let's see . . . how do we spend our time in Los Angeles? On the freeways. But how could I propose on a freeway?" he both asked and answered himself. Then it struck him.

"The radio . . . we listen to the radio on the freeways."

Mari thought he was acting oddly.

"Why are you taking the freeway to Beverly Hills?" Mari asked Bill, herself a seasoned driver who knew all the short-cuts, the canyons and bypasses.

Then—almost as if a robotized Bill had gotten a hidden signal—he promptly pulled the car to a stop on a ramp.

He turned up the volume on the radio, and got out.

Dumbfounded, Mari watched him walk in front of the car and open her door. He pulled a small box from his pocket, fell to one knee, and the two of them listened to a voice blasting from the radio:

"Love Songs on KOST FM now presents an important re-quest from Bill Cantos to Mari Falcone," said the announcer.

Bill's prerecorded voice said, "Mari . . . I love you . . . will you marry me?"

Almost one year from their first date together, mist sparkled in the corners of their eyes as Mari and Bill danced at their wedding—to the song that had been prescribed by each, for this very moment: "When I fall in love . . . it will be forever. . . ."

As Mari and Bill count the godwinks leading to their union in marriage, they continue to be astonished, but only for a moment, as they reacknowledge who's in charge of such things.

Summing up the meaning of godwinks in each of our lives, Mari recently composed a beautiful song, sweetly sung by Bill.

When God Winks at You
(Mari Falcone/©2003 Jolly Holiday Music ASCAP)

An unexpected phone call, a rainbow in the sky
The kindness of a stranger, a neighbor passing by
A goodness unimagined beyond what you can think
That's what happens—when God Winks.

A friend from many years ago, reappears again
That which seemed so far away, is now around the bend
A dream that was impossible, suddenly comes true
That's what happens—when God Winks at you.

It's a heavenly hello, a celestial connection
As you're wondering where to go
He's giving you direction.

So when you start to notice the most amazing things
Perhaps you need to stop and see, God's eyelash fluttering

His hope and reassurance are coming into view
That's what happens, that's what's happens
That's what happens—when God Winks at you.

The preceding stories exemplify that heavenly forces sometimes employ inanimate objects to help us to find—or even forget—our love experiences.

What is important here is that if you still struggle with the notion of a universe that is ordered and designed, these stories help you to conclude that there *is* a grand plan, and that in the end, all the pieces of the plan will sort themselves out in a beautiful way.

A word about romance

The only reason romance ever dies in a relationship is because we let it die. Both men and women need to take steps to assure that the flames of romance are always burning.

When Bruce went the extra distance to propose to Renee on television, in front of millions of witnesses, he was doing something very romantic. So was Bill when he proposed to Mari on the radio through a prearranged setup with the radio station.

Knowing both couples, I know the romance never died there. It continues on and on. A surprise bouquet of flowers to her, for no reason at all, or a candlelit room to greet him when he arrives home.

We need to say the words "I love you" several times every day to our mate, but we need to show it daily as well. That's romance.

When Louise goes on a trip and I am unable to accompany her, I hide little notes in her luggage. She calls me incessantly to remind me that she misses me terribly.

It really doesn't take all that much to keep a candle lit. Nor the romance alive.

10

Little Serendipities

"Coincidences are God's way of showing He has a sense of humor."

I've heard that quite a bit.

Also: "They are God's way of remaining anonymous."

It stands to reason that the maker of joy would have a joyful side. That's how it appears when we look at the way godwinks pop into our lives, sometimes like playful little serendipities.

The Cheethamses—that's incredible!

The two couples from Great Britain met on a trip to the Mediterranean. Both introduced themselves as Albert and Betty.

One had the last name Cheetham. The other, Rivers.

They laughed upon learning that Betty Rivers's maiden name was Cheetham. And Betty Cheetham's maiden name was Rivers.

They gasped upon learning that both couples were married at the same time, on the same day: 2 P.M., August 15, 1942.

They rolled their eyes when they concluded that both couples had two sons born in the same years, who had produced five grandchildren for each couple.

Both Bettys were aghast to find that they both worked for the post office.

Both Alberts were dumbfounded to learn that they both worked for the railway.

They were astonished to note that both Bettys were wearing 1930s bracelets, and each confessed to losing their engagement rings.

But they were, by this time, not surprised one bit to learn, even though they had just met, that their holidays were booked identically; both couples were to fly back to Britain on the same day.

See? God does have a sense of humor.

Kane and Dick:
how never to forget your spouse's birthday

"Get ready . . . I met the man I plan to marry," Kane told her mother following her first date with Dick White.

That was not the only incredible thing she learned about the man, ten years older than she, who asked her to dance, then swept her off her feet. Kane and Dick discovered that they were born *exactly* ten years apart—their birthdays are identical: August 30.

Not only that, they were born at the same hospital, Columbia-Presbyterian, in New York City.

If that's not enough, the same doctor delivered them both: Dr. Virgil Damon.

It was a summer weekend in the Hamptons, the playground for twenty-year-old college girls like Kane, and thirty-year-old ad agency executives like Dick.

"Where do you work?" asked Dick, making conversation.

"A doctor's office in New York," replied Kane.

"Hey . . . I know two doctors in New York," said Dick, just a little too enthusiastically. "One named Rosen, the other named Morris."

"I work for Morris."

"Really? Dr. Bob Morris?"

"Yes. Bob Morris."

There were over 15,000 doctors listed in the New York phone directory. But Kane and Dick were associated with just one of them; that is, other than their mutual obstetrician.

Just over seven months later, Obstetrician Dr. Virgil Damon raised a toast at a dinner on the eve of the couple's wedding. He reminded the two families gathered there that, collectively, they had an even greater investment in him than they first imagined. For he delivered not only Kane, but her two sisters, as well. And, he delivered not only Dick, but his two brothers, too.

Reflecting on her quick judgment to marry Dick forty-two years earlier, Kane says, "I have learned to respect my intuitive sense. Even harder—surrendering to it."

As for Dick, he knows he'll always remember his wife's birthday. Unless he forgets his own.

Parallel wedding winks across the Atlantic

Parallel stories of extraordinary coincidence between a pair of couples on each side of the Atlantic are astonishing.

After meeting at a yacht club in Rochester, New York, the Antonellis and the Partilos discovered many similarities between their weddings. As they began digging into their memories, they learned that not only had both couples met at a now defunct restaurant called Joe's Chop House, but both were married at the same time on the same day—noon, on May 4, 1968—with each bride accompanied by bridesmaids dressed in peach gowns.

The Antonellis and Partilos then each traveled to Miami Beach—driving more than twenty hours—for their honeymoons at the same resort. They never met because ten days of rain kept everyone in their rooms.

As if weather hadn't rained enough on their special event,

both couples were unable to show the pictures of their weddings—remarkably, both lost their wedding albums to the floods of Hurricane Agnes in 1972.

Thank goodness they met, in order to discover all these godwinks in their lives because, today, the Antonellis and Partilos are best of friends. And—in a way—neighbors: The Rochester Yacht Club, which both couples joined, unwittingly assigned them to adjoining slips for their boats.

A parallel story unfolded in England.

Elaine Reeves received invitations for two weddings to take place on the same day in July 2002. Imagine her shock when she read that both grooms, whom she knew, were to marry a young woman named Rachel Hodgkinson. And they both had the same middle name, Elizabeth.

She later learned that both couples—Rachel and Andrew, and Rachel and Adam—had decided upon the charming Upper House in Bariaston for their reception. Rachel and Adam got there first, so Rachel and Andrew chose a nearby venue for their postnuptial party.

By careful planning, and the good fortune of proximity, Elaine was able to attend both weddings and both receptions—and to meet both Rachel Elizabeth Hodgkinsons.

See what I mean? Godwinks come in all sizes and shapes. Sometimes they make you think you're seeing double.

Duffy's: two times two, times two, equals . . .

Sean Duffy is an identical twin. He met and married Maxine, who is also an identical twin.

Quite by coincidence, Sean's twin brother Darren met Maxine's twin sister Helen. They were married.

When they all got together and compared notes they found something shocking: all four of them were born in Oldham Hospital, Manchester, England, on exactly the same day, January 26, 1976.

Then both wives learned they were pregnant. The two babies were born in the same hospital as their parents, two weeks apart.

The ginger cookie wedding

Finally, I want to share a story that will pale in comparison to other godwink recitations in this chapter, but is, I believe, robust with serendipity.

When Louise and I decided to get married we went through all the questions every couple asks, such as: Where will we hold the ceremony? A significant question because our families were spread from Boston to Tampa, and Rochester to L.A. Meanwhile, our home was on an island off the coast of Cape Cod.

We also asked, what are the costs? Who will stay where? Who will sit next to whom? Yikes.

After wrestling with these issues for some time, we asked, "What is really important in a wedding ceremony, anyway?"

Our vows, we concluded. To each other, and to our Maker. Everything else was frosting on the cake.

So, we decided to get married—just the two of us, the preacher, and a witness—in a small church in Pawling, New York. It was a church that held considerable sentimentality. When I first went there I learned the godwink that my hero, Dr. Norman Vincent Peale, had a country home across the street. And when he died, he was buried behind the white-steepled, picture-postcard structure that looked over rolling hills and mountains.

Moreover, my topic as a guest speaker on Sunday morning had led to the birth of my first book, *When God Winks*.

Once decided, I said to Louise, "As our witness, let's invite Belle Reynolds, the sweet little lady who lives next to the church."

Belle was legendary for making the best ginger cookies in the north country and was known for handing them out in Ziploc-ed bags to just about everybody, for any event.

"Belle will bring the ginger cookies and that will take care of catering," I joked.

Before long people began asking about our wedding. When I explained that they were not invited—that in fact, no one was—I'd tell about Belle Reynolds.

As things developed, we were delighted with our no-hassle, no-expense, put-priorities-first wedding. Then, two weeks before the big day, I received a call from a *New York Times* reporter. She said her name was Lois Smith Brady.

"What's this I've heard about a ginger cookie wedding?" she inquired. "Can we come?"

"Sure," I replied, explaining what it was all about. But, inside, I was saying it differently: "Oh surrrrre . . . *The New York Times* is going to cover our bare-church wedding. Hah."

But they did.

The photographer got lost trying to find the little country church on top of the mountain, but Lois Smith Brady arrived, took my old Pentax with the broken light meter—vintage Cro-Magnon—and clicked off photos like a born paparazzo.

She got one lucky shot: Louise and myself, seated next to Belle Reynolds in the front pew of an empty church, crunching on Belle's blue-ribbon ginger cookies.

How did Ms. Brady of the *Times* know about our little wedding?

Beats me. Must have been a serendipitous godwink.

11

Six Words to Successful Relationships

The wonderful couples in this book who were united or re-united through unbelievable godwinks have left us with compelling insights on what makes a great relationship. Following are six words that have been redundantly spoken by them. When these six words are put together, their first letters spell another word.

Meanwhile, whether your soul mate has yet to appear on your radar screen, or whether he or she is on the other side of the bed, these pearls of wisdom are worth committing to memory and daily use, as soon as possible.

Laughter

Paula and Gary Conover, and Hillary and Bill Kimmelman underscored the importance of humor as a common thread to hold themselves together as couples.

Moreover, during those tense moments that invariably arise in relationships, if one partner or the other can provoke laughter, stress is released, and the potential for disagreement dissipates.

Appreciation

The Arvella and Robert Schuller story highlights the importance of expressing genuine appreciation for each other.

Don't let the sun set on any day without expressing and reexpressing heartfelt appreciation for things, even the very smallest things, that your partner has done.

Understanding

"You don't *listen* to me."

The person who says that really means: "You may be listening with your ears, but you aren't *understanding* what I am trying to communicate."

Successful couples like Debrah and Greg Hoblit have found ways to show that they are clearly paying attention to each other. One method is to repeat what their partner has just said, in different words to show, as Greg says, that we are "really hearing."

God

Pauletta and Denzel Washington built their relationship on the rock-solid foundation of mutual faith.

Their marriage works, they say, because it is not just be-tween the two of them—it is a commitment of three, with God in the middle.

A rope with three cords woven together, is stronger than with two.

Hold

Does the meaning of the marriage vow "to have and to hold" mean to physically hold, as in hug?

I have come to conclude that *hold* really means to "hold up"—to honor. To place your partner in a higher position than you place yourself.

Ask any couple in this book, "Who is the most important person in your relationship?" and they are likely to say: "He is. No, she is."

Support

Kimberly and Jerry's, and Alice and Jack's stories each exem-plified that we all need to have someone we can rely on. Someone we can trust will be watching our backs. To catch us if we fall. To provide a shoulder to cry on. We need to know that our partner is there to support us. Never to tear us down—especially in front of others—but to build us up. To give us constant messages of support.

Love Laughs

Now, when you put those Six Key Words for a Successful Relationship together, you get:

> Laughter
> Appreciate
> Understand
> God
> Hold
> Support

It's a mnemonic device used by Louise and myself in a seminar we do, mentioned earlier, "LOVE LAUGHS: Everything I Know about Wrecking Relationships I Learned in My Last Marriage!"

Conclusion

Coming from the broadcast school of thought, to "tell your listeners what you're going to tell them . . . tell them . . . then, tell them what you've told them," I am hopeful that this review of the salient points in this book will be helpful. And hopeful.

More than anything else, when you put this book down, it is my wish that you will have hope; hope that if you are not yet connected with your perfect love, that you will be. That your faith, bolstered by the hopeful stories you've read here, will carry you on to the perfect fit in the jigsaw puzzle of life that has been destined for you.

And that if you have found your perfect love, it is my wish that the words of wisdom shared by others will keep your relationship fresh and exciting.

Let's have another look as I paraphrase some key points:

You are part of a perfect world

We *do* live in a perfect universe. . . .

Think about how almost all of life on earth is sustained by the perfect harmony of the seasons, the sun, and the cycles of life.

Letting your mind's eye focus on the image of a newborn child, seeing those five little fingers and five tiny toes . . . you are looking at the creation of harmonious perfection.

That little person is you.

So . . . if perfection exists in that which is as large as the universe and as miniature as your baby toe, why wouldn't it also be likely that God has created a perfect design for your life that includes a perfect soul mate?

In Yiddish there is a word: *bashert*. It means "your intended one."

Godwinks and love

"When it comes to decisions about love, I bring people back to my original premise: godwinks are like the silent messages you received as a kid from Grandma across the dining-room table—quiet communications of support and reassurance—through a little wink.

That wink said: "Hey kid, I'm thinking about you right now. I love you. Hang in there."

That wink did *not* say, "Have another piece of pie." Or, "Help yourself to the mashed potatoes."

That wink was *not* a directive for you.

It was a reassuring communication of love *affirming* that you had the support of someone who loved you, in the choices that *you* were making.

Godwink links

You can probably think of many times in your own life where, had it not been for that "chance" meeting with that *very* person at that *very* moment, your life would have gone into a distinctly different direction.

You may even conclude that those encounters were godwinks.

But, rather than looking at those experiences from *your* perspective and outcome, I want you to focus on *the person who just "happened" to come your way.* What caused *them* to be there at that very instant? To become radically involved in the direction of your life at that precise point in time?

Is it possible that they were divinely directed?

Is it possible that without their consciously knowing it, they were unwitting messengers of godwinks to you?

I believe that we are *all* unwitting messengers at one time or another—what I call "Godwink Links"—in the lives of others; emissaries of joy, rarely realizing what a wonderful role we are fulfilling.

You may have been the reason someone connected with a new career, a new spiritual awakening, or new love in their life. You were a Godwink Link.

Your Godwink Link may be near

The man or woman who fulfills your every desire for a deep, lasting love may also arrive into your midst through a God-wink Link.

Look around you. Perhaps someone who is unknowingly being employed as an angel on earth is already in your presence.

Explore your past to find your godwink map

When you reach threshold moments in your life, those times when you experience an event, encounter someone, or make a life-changing decision setting you onto an entirely new path, there are always godwinks, like signs at the fork in a road. You may notice them and shrug them off. Or you may be so involved in the new experience that you fail to notice them altogether.

But, they are there.

When you do a sort of archaeological expedition into your past, first recalling the threshold moments, then thinking about godwinks that you overlooked or forgot about, you can map them.

Mapping godwinks to see the big picture

When you look back on your life, with the clarity of hindsight, you'll see patterns of signposts or godwinks at certain points, as you moved from one place to another. What emerges is a marvelous mosaic of free will and God's will.

You come to better understand that you are on a sort of Global Positioning System that has helped you to navigate through life.

Someone is listening

We so often wonder: How do I really know there's somebody up there watching over me? With six billion people on this planet, how can I be sure that my voice is getting through?

Mapping your godwinks and seeing how your life has followed a more orderly path than you may have imagined will reassure that your voice *does* get through.

Hold an expectation of fulfillment

Starting every day with the expectation that it is going to be a great day is different than *hoping* it will be.

That's the mind-set I would like you to adapt. Go into every day with the total expectation that the desires of your heart are *going* to be fulfilled, that you are *going* to achieve the goals that you've set for yourself, and that you are *going* to find the love that you deserve.

Adapt this as your habit, and you can expect many unexpected godwinks!

Letting go and letting God

When you let go, you no longer perseverate about not finding your ideal mate. You instead put your desires out there, out of mind, and wait for the perfect circumstances to appear.

When you do meet someone and strong feelings come over you, ask if this is really love, or just infatuation. Is this the real thing, or my desire to *be* in love?

Remember, in the jigsaw puzzle of your life there is a perfect piece destined to fit perfectly with you. But jamming together two pieces that look like they kind of fit, but don't, never works.

The need for certainty

We need to feel certain that we are safe. When we're uncertain about our safety, we worry.

We need to feel certain that we will not lose our source of income. If we're uncertain, we worry.

And, we desire the certainty and security of someone to

love ... someone who equally loves us. When our perfect match has not yet materialized, we are uncertain, and it's worrisome.

But the signs of affirmation that come with godwinks will help you eradicate uncertainty and worry. Often the signs are right there in front of you and you fail to see them. In your daily life, your mind can become so clouded with anxiety, that you to totally miss seeing the reaffirming signs of encouragement.

The small voice within

"You must continue to listen to the small still voice within—your intuition—and make the important choices in your life on your own, bolstered by an awareness that you are surrounded by the invisible safety net of the Almighty, confirmed by godwinks, that you are never alone.

Godwinks as signposts

Signposts don't choose where you go.

You do.

But once you make your determination, the signposts are there to support your decision.

That's the role of godwinks in your life. They are signposts *affirming* that you are heading in the right direction; reassuring that you're getting closer to your goal; reminding you to stay within boundaries; and bolstering the choices *you* have made.

Louise & SQuire

THEN...

Louise and I officially met on the set of ABC TV's *Kaptain Kool & the Kongs* in 1974.

...AND NOW

Today, many godwinks later, we are perfect soul mates, deliriously in love.